Craic Baby

DARACH Ó SÉAGHDHA is the author of the popular twitter account @theirishfor, whose followers include Dara Ó Briain, Ed Byrne, Gerry Adams, Amy Huberman, the Rubberbandits, Colm O'Regan and Gráinne Seoige. He lives in Swords, Co. Dublin and is married, with one daughter.

Also by Darach Ó Séaghdha

Motherfoclóir

CRAIC BABY

Dispatches from a rising language

Darach Ó Séaghdha

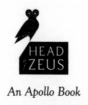

An Apollo Book

This is an Apollo book, first published in the UK in 2018
by Head of Zeus Ltd

9 7 5 3 2 4 6 8

A catalogue record for this book is available from
the British Library.

ISBN (HB): 9781788545259
ISBN (E): 9781788545273

Designed and typeset by Lindsay Nash

Printed and bound in Great Britain
by CPI Group (UK) Ltd, Croydon CR0 4YY

Head of Zeus Ltd
First Floor East
5–8 Hardwick Street
London EC1R 4RG
WWW.HEADOFZEUS.COM

For Erin, my Northern star

An sgéal fada ní hé is fearr
The longest tale is not the best

ANON, FIFTEENTH CENTURY

CONTENTS

AUTHOR'S NOTE

As with *Motherfoclóir*, this book is not intended to teach Irish or to defend or denounce state policies pertaining to the Irish language in the Republic of Ireland and Northern Ireland. It's not that I don't care about such policies; on the contrary. If someone could promise me that by writing that book I could end all those rehearsed, repetitive conversations forever, I'd write it. But nobody will make or keep that promise.

What I've decided to do with the *Motherfoclóir* podcast is to talk to people about their own personal relationships with Irish, people with different levels of fluency and varying backgrounds. We've had conversations about how the Irish language interacts with technology, with the legal system, its use online and offline. We've chatted with Irish speakers living abroad and Irish speakers who've come from far away.

We've had the kinds of conversations that don't always make it to mainstream radio, due to a pathological need to only ever ask about 'the way it's taught' and the costs involved. For me, that approach is like having the panellists after every football match discuss nothing but the offside rule – even though that's what they discussed last week, and the week before. And even though everybody watching knows their position on it already.

My hope is that people will enjoy this book regardless of their level of Irish (and maybe someone who hasn't used their Irish since school might be tempted to dip their toe back in, possibly even book themselves in to an evening class), but also that we might be able to change the conversation a little bit. We can have better discussions about Irish and catch the attention of people who might otherwise tune out.

Darach Ó Séaghdha

P.S. For narrative purposes, in some instances people mentioned in this book have had their names changed or merged.

INTRODUCTION

In March 2016 I was floating on a cloud. My wife and I had just moved into our first home. I had found a literary agent and was on the brink of signing a book deal. And most importantly of all, we were expecting our first child and we already knew it was a little girl.

The night before she was born, Erin and I wondered together what kind of person our daughter would grow up to be. Clever and beautiful, of course. Would she go to university in Dublin like her father, or Belfast like her mother?* She would definitely start learning to drive earlier than her parents, who both left it ridiculously late.

And obviously she would go to the Gaelscoil up the road – that wasn't even up for discussion. Our generation had been told how useless and pointless Irish was, but now our friends were telling us about their kids speaking Irish to each other on the way home from school. It didn't seem

* Erin never warmed to the familiar form 'Mam', popular in the Republic.

to be out of reach. None of these things seemed to be out of reach. All she needed was a name and a birthday.

This conversation would come to haunt me over the following days.

Shortly after Lasairíona was born, we were told that she had Down syndrome. This was not information we had prepared for, and neither of us had any relevant experience or knowledge to hear it as other than bad news. Our ignorance cast a shadow over this wonderful event, the arrival of our long-hoped-for daughter.

The temptation to give up on the outside world was very strong. But Erin insisted that I not throw away my first serious opportunity to get published, so I pressed down hard on my feelings and kept writing.

Down syndrome isn't an incapacity like blindness or deafness; it's a different kind of normal. It makes people more vulnerable to some illnesses and less vulnerable to others. Certain developmental milestones can happen later, but not always. As new parents you discover that you have a baby with an extra chromosome, but you don't yet know how that will express itself. Anytime over the next few months when something doesn't happen the way you expect it to, you're not sure if it's because of your child's condition or if she's just growing at her own pace. Waiting for the other shoe to drop builds a tension inside you.

By mid-June, I was following a rigid rota of appointments with specialists, nappy changes and night feeds, a routine that was beginning to feel like normality. With so much going on that made me feel helpless and useless, there was a real satisfaction in ticking off small chores. We were processing the news of the diagnosis in different ways, and I think now that the hectic business of meeting publishers to pitch my book was keeping me from breaking down completely.

With all this going on, I was really looking forward to having lunch with Frances, a writer friend who had recently returned from Oxford. As we caught up over a lunchtime pint near Stephen's Green, I was interrupted by a phone call from my agent. I had an offer for my book. After the phone call had ended, I remember looking around at passers-by, astonished that they were just walking the streets as if it was an ordinary day.

In the way of great friends, Frances was even more excited than I was. Friends can enjoy each other's good news without being doomed to retell it endlessly – which frees them to go bananas when you can't.

Once I convinced her that I had no more details to give, we spoke of other matters. Our neighbours the British were having a referendum. They weren't as experienced at them as we were, and it looked like this one was going to flop just as the recent plebiscites on Scottish independence and alternative voting had. Still, no country in Europe over the previous decade had had a successful European referendum first time around (Ireland had re-run two of them).

The next day was like a bad dream. Not for the last time in 2016, sadly, my lifelong love of watching election results became a kind of ironic punishment. Brexit had begun and I was actively worried about the world into which I had brought a child.

Perversely, there was a wealth of engaged debate about the value of the European Union and its institutions in the days after the referendum result, more so than in the weeks before the vote. Two things rapidly became apparent. First, the very existence of Ireland had not been part of the Brexit vision – the presence of a land border, the delicate issues surrounding the Good Friday Agreement, the difference between how the Northern Irish public voted and how some of their politicians did had all been ignored – and this blindness would surely come home to roost for the most ardent supporters of leaving the EU.

Second, if a famously cautious electorate such as the British could commit such an atrocious act of self-harm in the pursuit of a white nationalist Tír na nÓg, could the Americans do the same? At this stage, Trump* was still a ridiculous and hideous prospect. Among the many, many warnings about his character was an incident in which he performed a grotesque, mocking imitation of a reporter with a disability.

* *Luaman* (an old Irish word for a small hand) hasn't been included in modern dictionaries. I smell a conspiracy.

The Trump and Brexit votes, both taking pollsters by surprise, were attributed to a visceral reaction against those progressive niceties often grouped under political correctness – health and safety, protections for workers and consumers, sensitive phrasing to replace hurtful or unhelpful words – as well as the trade and migration arrangements negotiated to make war less likely. In America and Britain, older voters reached for an idealized past that was out of their grasp. They were like Oisín on his return from Tír na nÓg: the home he missed didn't exist anymore, and he could never go back.

I held Lasairíona in my arms and reflected on all we had taken for granted about the world even in those dark moments of coming to terms with her diagnosis. I had always assumed that awareness of medical conditions was increasing, and that those imperfect peace treaties were grudgingly accepted because the people who knew how they worked knew that they worked. The idea that there could be an armed checkpoint separating my half-Northern Irish baby from her grandparents was moving from an impossibility to an inevitability with sickening speed. If the Irish economy could be damaged by a neighbour's tantrum, would our government choose to cut services for boys and girls like her?

Then she ran her tiny fingers through my beard and smiled at me. She wanted me to know something.

What do we talk about when we talk about Irish? When we talk about saving or supporting a language, do we mean the musical combination of syllables, or something more profound?

Something I've been asked a bit since Lasairíona was born is why I still care about the Irish language when I have 'real problems' now. Surely Gaeilge, for all its charms, isn't a hardship issue for anyone? Don't the services that children with Down syndrome require matter more, and deserve more of my attention?

Rather than be led into a simple answer (which would make this a much shorter book), I say: there is an overlap between the two, and my heart beats in that overlap.

In both cases, with the heritage of minority languages and the potential of people with disabilities, there is resistance against an imposed concept of normality – the idea that people are supposed to look and behave a particular way, and that people who cannot or do not are some kind of inconvenience. While many of us are normal in many parts of our lives, we all have parts of our bodies or our character where the world reminds us are not normal.

Sometimes it's the built environment. Something as simple as the height of a table or the placement of a door can quietly tell you that a room was designed without someone like you in mind. Sometimes it's a word that carries a legacy of assumptions and hurt more familiar to you than the person who utters it. And sometimes it's the taste of your own silence as you listen to people with a platform explain why your wants and needs aren't important, aren't economically viable or bother someone else.

Craic Baby picks up exactly where *Motherfoclóir* left off. It explores the very new and very old parts of the Irish language from a personal perspective. While my first book was steeped in memory and a father-son relationship, this

one hinges on the beginning of a father-daughter relationship, and how watching a child learn to communicate
changes how you think about language.

A Fada Can Make All the Difference

Feire	groove or lip
Féire	crookedness
Gráín	cuddle
Gráin	hatred or abhorrence
Ar	on, at, in
Ár	slaughter

NORMAL PEOPLE

The Irish word for man is **fear**. Now that I was a father, fear was omnipresent. From the hours before her birth onwards, I was pointedly conscious of my own particularly male uselessness against the swirling chaos around me.

On my first full day minding Lasairíona on my own, I put her in her pram – a Batmobile compared to the yoke I was wheeled around in back in 1978 – and took her for a walk to the village. Taking a short cut through a nearby estate, the footpath was blocked by parked cars. I grumbled to myself and reluctantly pushed her along the road for a bit. When I attempted to join the footpath in the next part of the estate, I noticed it wasn't actually wide enough to accommodate the pram.

Then it struck me: if it's like this for a pram-pusher, what must it be like for a person in a wheelchair?

I was noticing the design of the world around me more than ever before – the amount of personal space considered normal, font sizes in newspapers and signs, the availability of audio description features or subtitles on certain TV shows, objects a baby could and couldn't reach. I started thinking about all the things that could go wrong. Every time I saw a 'baby on board' sticker I was reminded of the horrible origins of those cute little signs.*

And I really started noticing the way we use language.

At some point in those early months I made a bland, obvious comment in some conversation I was barely a part of, and someone else said, 'Well, duh.' I had never given that expression any thought before, but suddenly I found myself thinking about its origins. The only satisfying explanation was that it was an attempt to mockingly imitate someone with a disability that affected their speech. I reflected on my own use of the phrase in the past and decided I didn't want to use it anymore.

* In the pre-car seat days, 'baby on board' stickers were originally intended to advise paramedics to look for a baby in the event of a car crash.

The Irish for political correctness is **ceartaiseacht pholaitiúil**. Rather than matching 'correctness' exactly, *ceartaiseacht* is listed in the *foclóir* as:

Insistence on one's rights.
Self-righteousness.
Conceit, priggishness.

I can't help feeling the translator is editorializing here. This is understandable; in English, the term is only used by critics of what it represents. While it was briefly used in the 1970s to refer to unpopular positions taken by a group purely on the grounds of being consistent with their core policies, this had ceased by the time the expression entered the mainstream. Every American presidency brings its own vocabulary (WMD, fake news, wiretapping, drone and what the meaning of 'is' is), and political correctness is intimately associated with the reign of George H. W. Bush, who frequently used it to dismiss critics.

I was all too conscious of the PC bogeyman and the carbon copy replies my peers gave when their actions or words were challenged – free speech, political correctness has gone too far, it's hard to keep up with all that terminology, no need to be offended on behalf of people who can speak for themselves, and so on. I wanted people to know how I felt about the term (I wasn't too keen on the word 'karma' as appropriated by Westerners either – that's a different day's work), but I really didn't want to scold or shame anyone, put them on the spot or start fights. Most of all, I didn't want anyone to politely agree with me and then tell their mates what they really thought after I left.

These thoughts were on my mind when I started to produce the *Motherfoclóir* podcast after submitting my first book. After being a guest on a different show on the Headstuff Podcast Network, it occurred to me that the format was ideal for expanding on some of the ideas I had touched on in *Motherfoclóir*, as well as giving a voice to some of the remarkable people I had become aware of through my rediscovery of Irish in the social media age. Ostensibly we'd talk about Irish, but the real conversations were about the place of Irish in people's lives, the relationships they had with it and the role it played in modern Irish society. My contributors and I would bat ideas around and discuss how we'd incorporate them into a half-hour podcast, and that's when I heard about orthographic depths.

One of the contributors on the show is a remarkable PhD student named Gearóidín McEvoy, who has dyslexia. This condition would have entitled her to an exemption from studying Irish in secondary school if she had asked for it. However, she told me that while she struggled with English spelling and pronunciation forms (why don't 'hood' and 'moon' rhyme, for example), she never struggled this way with Irish. It was, she said, the first language that didn't try to trick her.

This is because Irish is shallow and English is deep, in terms of orthography. In a nutshell, orthographic depth measures how likely speakers are to be able to pronounce a word they haven't seen before, based on a language's conventions. Finnish is one of the shallowest (most faithful to its own rules), English one of the deepest – there is no specific grammatical rule explaining why the silent g in 'sign' gets pronounced in the related word 'signature'.

Talking about perceptions of dyslexia and of Irish on the show, she made a point that startled me: if she hadn't studied Irish, she might not have developed the love of languages that went on to open so many doors for her – teaching in different countries, working in translation and much more. Irish has grammatical rules and spelling conventions like any other language, and it actually sticks to them fairly well once you know them.

I was so used to hearing Irish described as difficult and capricious that the notion that it might actually be a lifeline to a student struggling with other parts of school hadn't been presented to me before. This was especially interesting in regard to another visibility issue.

Some time previous to this, a woman called Sinéad Burke had contacted me. Sinéad is a blogger, activist, lecturer and much, much more, and a huge part of her work involves addressing perceptions of disability and talking about her own experience of having achondroplasia, standing three feet, five inches tall. As with many conditions, the informal terminology surrounding this is fraught with words that are hurtful or unhelpful; while some little people accept the word 'dwarf', others do not. And none appreciate the word 'midget'.

She used a line that really stuck with me: it is not her achondroplasia that makes her feel disabled, but the built environment of the world around her that does not include her – the height of sinks, steps, door handles and so many more things.

Sinéad told me about her Leaving Cert Irish oral exam, and the discomfort she felt going in. She knew she was going to have to talk about herself, but she didn't want to use the word **abhac**, the incumbent Irish word for dwarf, also listed as the word for midget. These were terms in English that she would not use, but if she used a term to describe herself that wasn't in the dictionary, she was concerned that she would be marked down in her exam.

After finding out the process for getting a new entry

added to the Irish terminology database, she successfully got **duine beag** (literally, little person) included. Among other things, this meant future Leaving Cert students wouldn't have the concerns she had going in.

The fact that the Irish language could open these doors was a source of great comfort and hope to me, and I wanted to look at all the ways the **teanga** – especially the spoken language – engages with the modern world: the changes in society, attitudes and technology. I wanted to consider where Irish was when I was a child, and where it will be when my daughter is an adult.

The Irish word for koala is **cóála**. Some people groan at the new loanwords for things that have not been a large part of Irish life, but I love this one because it has two fadas in a row, which is quite unusual. Generally, words with consecutive fadas are compounds, such as **spréóg**, which means little spark, formed by combining **spré** (a spark of typical size, but also wealth or a dowry) with the suffix -**óg** (small or young). Likewise, **croíán**, a playboy or lad-about-town, is derived from **croí**, heart.

Consecutive fadas in non-compound words are quite rare in Irish and tend to pop up in new words where re-phoneticization or a compound of existing words is required. There's a whole process involved, which we'll talk about next.

A Fada Can Make All the Difference

Lánn   **dawn (a form of láigh)**
Lann   blade

Grag   **grog**
Grág   shrivelled tree stump, or
               cawing sound

Mearaíocht   **going loo-laa**
Méaraíocht   fingering

NEW WORDS

~~~

The Republic of Ireland is proud of her neutrality, and there is no tomb to the unknown soldier here. However, I look forward to a tomb for the unknown translator: **an t-aistritheoir anaithnid**.

But another part of me doesn't want to wait for a tomb. Right now, I want to buy a pint for the humble legend in foclóir.ie who translated 'for fuck's sake' as **in ainm Dé** (in God's name). While searching for suitably interesting words to share with the followers of @theirishfor, I stumbled across a point that vexed me: the modern Irish dictionary had translations for the very problematic English terms jailbait (**siocair phríosúin**) and friend zone (**crios cairdis**), but no entry (yet) for mansplain. In my mind I put myself in the place of a dictionary or terminology database employee. Would I have the freedom to only translate words that I liked? If I had the power to turn down words I didn't like, what criteria would I use? As appealing as I find the idea of an Irish language **beo agus glan** (living and clean), without nasty words and their associated ideas, is this really the responsibility of the lexicographer?

For modern Irish, there's a terminology database (*an Bunachar Náisiúnta Téarmaíochta don Ghaeilge*, available online at www.tearma.ie) and an English-Irish dictionary (*An Foclóir Nua Béarla-Gaeilge*, available online at www. focloir.ie). They have different processes. The way we construct such permanent vocabularies and include new words expresses eloquently what we really think about Irish today. Where the words come from, how long they stay around, who gets to use them first and the processes involved all have to be considered.

⅄⅄⅄ Authenticity and Cromulence ⅄⅄⅄

*'Embiggened? I never heard that word before
I moved to Springfield'.
'I don't know why – it's a perfectly cromulent word'.*

THE SIMPSONS, 'LISA THE ICONOCLAST'

New objects and ideas keep getting invented, new events keep happening, and language has to keep up. When we encounter a phenomenon that hasn't been named yet (the sensation of leaving the iron or the gas ring on when you leave the house, for example, or avoiding an acquaintance at a bus stop so you can listen to your headphones instead of making agonizing small talk), we describe it using the words we already have. If the phenomenon turns out to be widespread or significant, somebody might coin an apt name for it. If that name is especially witty or succinct, it might catch on. If two people coin such a phrase and they both catch on, you just might have a new element of regional or generational slang.

It's hard to know why some words capture the mood of the moment and others don't, but authenticity is certainly a factor – or at least the appearance of authenticity. It needs to be a perfectly cromulent word.

The perceived origins of a word contribute to its authenticity, popularity and value. I wrote in *Motherfoclóir* about how certain loanwords to English have added force on account of the qualities associated with the language-culture they came from: the literal meaning of *verboten* is underlined by the Teutonic sternness, *ciao* carries Italian informality, and *kawaii* refers to a specifically Japanese kind of super-cuteness, utterly unlike the cute hoors of Ireland. So what qualities do we associate with words that come to Irish from English?

We can't talk about new Irish words without talking about the elephant in the room – the relationship modern Irish has with English, the number of loanwords attributable to English and the close similarity between the Irish and English words for the same thing. Speaking of elephants, let's start there: that's **eilifint*** in Irish. It's the same word as elephant, really, except the spelling reflects Irish

---

* The Irish for tusk is *starr*. There are two words for ivory in Irish: *eabhar* (sounds like ever) and *déad* (sounds like day-d).

pronunciation norms rather than English ones. This is also the case with the Irish for chimpanzee – **simpeansaí**.

Is this process worthwhile if the word is pretty much the same? This cuts to several key points about both Irish and English (neither elephant nor chimpanzee is found in *Beowulf* or Chaucer, after all). As loanwords to both languages, they make perfect case studies for the differences between English and Irish.

⅄⅄⅄ Consonant Followed by H ⅄⅄⅄

Chimpanzee and elephant both have consonant pairs ending with a h: ch and ph. This would signify a *séimhiú* in Irish, and could cause confusion. So the ph becomes an f (just like *fón* for phone) and the ch becomes an s (a shhh sound as in the beginning of *séimhiú*).

⅄⅄⅄⅄⅄⅄ Vowels ⅄⅄⅄⅄⅄⅄

The system of pronouncing vowels in English is so intricate that native speakers seldom think about it. In Irish, it's a little bit more transparent on account of the existence of fadas.

| **AE** | like ay | think *cupán tae* for a cup of tea |
| **AO** | like ay | such as in the famous grammar rule, *caol le caol* |

AÍ	like ee in seen	all those *prat_aí_*, potatoes, you've eaten
ÁI	like awi	we learned this when we were *p_ái_stí*, children
AI	like a in Andrew	found in *B_ai_le Átha Cliath*, Dublin
ÉA	like ai in pair/chair/stair	*aon sc_éa_l*, literally one story – means 'any news?'
EA	like yuh or ahh	*b_ea_g*, small or *bean*, woman
ÉI	like ei in reign, feign	*p_éi_re*, a pair
EI	like e in get, met, yet	remember *liom, leat, l_ei_s*
EO	like o in shove, or like yoh	*b_eo_* means alive, *f_eo_il* means meat that is no longer alive
IA	like ea in near, fear	*b_ia_,* food
ÍO	like ee in meek, cheek	*n_ío_r chreid sé*, he didn't believe
IO	like yuh	the boy's name F_io_nn
IÚ	like ew in new	surely your teacher yelled CI_Ú_NAS, demanding silence?

ÓI	like oi in going	a defender is a *cosantóir*
OI	like i in will	a forest or grove is *coill*
UA	like in truant	*bua*, triumph
ÚI	like in ruin	*súil* meaning eye, *siúil* meaning walk
UÍ	like ee in seem	*buí*, yellow
UI	like ui in quill	*an bhfuil cead agam*, may I?

⟂ Genitives, Plurals and Genitive Plurals ⟂

Another sensible reason for using Irish spelling conventions in loanwords is that it flags how to pronounce a word in different grammatical cases. English typically adds an s to the end of a word to indicate that the plural form is being applied. Irish also adjusts nouns to indicate plurals, but to indicate other grammatical states too.

Sure, **simpeansaí** sounds like chimpanzee. But two or more chimpanzees? The plural isn't *simpeansaís*, it's **simpeansaithe**. Multiple elephants would be eilifintí (or **na heilifintí**). Sometimes the loanword requires no tweaking at all, such as **bus** for bus (an abbreviation of omnibus, though only the most diehard pedants and retro-minded stylists spell it with an apostrophe, 'bus, anymore).

I'm sure a few people are reading this and thinking: Fair enough, Darach, but wouldn't it be better if these animals were given clever, pretty names that captured an Irish attitude to the world rather than just the phonetics?

I do have some sympathy for this view – it would be very fancy indeed if the Irish word for koala translated literally as *Giant Australian Tail-less Squirrel* or *Furry Eucalyptus Monster*.

However, imagine for a moment that you work in Dublin Zoo. You're preparing a bilingual press release about a baby gnu that needs to be out by 5pm, and it's already 3pm. You find there's no word for gnu in the dictionary. Do you stick the word 'gnu' in, or do you sit back and contemplate the singular charms of that beast, seeing if you can draw parallels between it and the creatures from Irish mythology that it most closely resembles, possibly trying to make a pun on the name of a public figure with gnu-like qualities? Do you assume that the people reading this new word will know what you're on about?

I daresay you'd just use the word gnu, checking that it doesn't already mean something rude in Irish. This explains the co-existence of loanwords (**ar mo bhisicle**) with considered translations (**ar mo rothar**).

Having said that, if you were writing a children's book set in Dublin Zoo with a cast of adorable Irish-speaking animals, you'd be well within your rights to come up with a creative name for a koala or a gnu, and if it really caught on, it could claim a place in the dictionary. The Irish translation of *The Little Prince* has **nathair boa** (boa snake) for boa constrictor, even though **buachrapaire** is in the *foclóir*,

and I'm fairly certain that the translator hasn't been arrested yet.*

A favourite example of this is
Tliongánach, the Irish word for Klingon, which I presume was coined in

* Well, not in
respect of that
incident anyway.

the context of some fan fiction. It's nice to know that when
translating this one, someone cared enough to recognize
that Klingon is an exonym (a word outsiders use to describe
a place or people) and thus base the transliteration on that
language's own word for itself (*tlhIngan*). This is consistent
with the Irish word for Swiss, **Eilvéiseach**, being based on
Helvetica rather than on Switzerland. **Tliongánach** stands
up well compared to a science fiction neologism such as
Jedíoch (Jedi), which doesn't even replace that terribly
déclassé J.

ᚔᚔᚔᚔ **Banging on the Door** ᚔᚔᚔᚔᚔ

Culture eats strategy for breakfast, as they say in work
training courses. This is business-speak for the old story of
the scorpion and the frog that you'll know from *Drive* and
The Crying Game: a scorpion's true nature will win out over
its logical self-interest. Because Irish is a minority language
and one of the states covering the area where it is spoken
has an interest in promoting it, there's a strategic element
which seeks to interact with the cultural aspects.

As with other minority languages, certain Irish words
and terms are generated on request, as with **duine beag**
for little person. I met a Welsh university lecturer last year

who told me that a project he had been working on was responsible for adding eighteen new words to the Welsh language. As these words all referred to his field – regulations regarding ancillary electrical goods with particular regard to their universality – it was unlikely that they were going to slide into common speech. After all, the English terms certainly hadn't. However, the regulations and devices he was dealing with would interact with human beings at some level, and those frustrations and features would generate slang terms or clever nicknames.

Here are some examples of new words where a little thought paid off nicely.

Ceárta is an older word suitable for upcycling: it means a forge or a workshop, and can be used figuratively to refer to a centre of activity or gossip (much like water cooler). An actual water cooler would be **fuaraitheoir uisce** in Irish.

Another is **uighleach**. This one isn't in modern dictionaries yet, but might be a good candidate for the Irish translation of 'toxic masculinity' – it has two possible translations into English, which are 'manly' and 'dung or manure'.

Twitter threads – a new genre of journalism where someone replies to their own tweet repeatedly to create a long-form piece, compelling the author to say something interesting in each 280-character chunk – are the ballads of our age. That is to say, many of them are too long and their ability to inform public policy is debatable.

However, anyone in the decades to come who is doomed to write a thesis on the 2010s will surely have to address their impact. If that thesis is in Irish, what will it be called? The general term for thread is **snáth**, but it has been suggested that with specific regard to Twitter threads, **sraith** (row or series) could be used. Using **sraith** would be a cheeky nod to the **sraith pictiúr** – the comic strips that Leaving Cert students get to chat about in their oral exams.

You may have experienced sphenopalatine ganglioneuralgia without realizing it – you probably called it something like brain freeze, or ice-cream (or margarita) headache. Until recently, this was one of the most notorious entries in the Irish terminology database: **tinneas cinn de dheasca bia fuar a ithe**. Translated literally, this is 'a headache from eating cold food', which is more of a description than a name.

I can't prove this but I suspect that there may have been a reluctance to add wimpy words to the Irish language, which is a language for people who are tough. Triskaidekaphobia, another condition that would never have bothered the hard men of 1916, is **fóibe roimh an uimhir trí déag** – literally, a phobia of the number thirteen. Perhaps we're not as macho anymore: in 2018, a more tailored entry for brain freeze, **reo inchinne** (brain frost), was added.

The Irish word for country, **tír**, is pronounced like the English word tear, a drop of sadness from the eye. The affairs of world nations and their leaders certainly give me occasion to confuse the two, not least on this island where I live. I'm an utterly South Dublin boy who found himself married to an utterly Northern Irish woman, a girl who grew up down the road from the Giant's Causeway and the disappearing lake. We'd laugh about the small differences between our international phone codes and our perceptions of each other: she a constituent of the Paisley dynasty, I a Southerner unable to pronounce 'th' sounds correctly (or anything resembling what she considered to be correct). It never really occurred to us that after obtaining and holding such an elusive détente, world events would shove a wedge between our native jurisdictions on a whim.

The Irish for crocodile is **crogall**, which is word-neighbour in the dictionary with **cróga**, meaning brave. This came up in 2017 when Arlene Foster made a remark regarding an Irish Language Act which I'm sure she regretted – she appropriated a Winston Churchill quote about negotiating with Nazis when she compared conceding to the demands of Sinn Féin and other groups for such legislation to feeding a crocodile. This neat visual image allowed disagreement to her views to crystallize and effectively gave the protests a theme.

Northern Ireland has had a frustrating struggle turning its hard-won peace into business-as-usual politics, and the events surrounding Brexit* haven't really helped.

---

* It's been pointed out that *Sasamach* as a translation for Brexit, while terribly droll, is inaccurate as it only refers >>

Something often commented on in relation to the North is the inability to agree on a vocabulary for the same things:

Na Sé Chontae – the six counties

Tuaisceart Éireann – Northern Ireland

Tuaisceart na hÉireann – North of Ireland

Ulaidh – Ulster

An Próiseas Síochána – the Peace Process

This granularity of terminology isn't terribly new: Donegal has two names in Irish, *Tír Chonaill* (literally, Conall's Land) and *Dún na nGall* (literally, Fort of the Foreigners).

One of the places where new Irish words have to be identified or constructed at speed is on the Irish language news services. In order to do this properly, strict conventions are used. Names of international figures such as politicians are

>> to England (*Sasanach* meaning an English person). I understand this to actually be the point – it's a comment on the English nationalism underpinning the Brexit moment and the strong Remain vote in Scotland and Northern Ireland. Furthermore, Brexit isn't accurate either – it's the UK (political entity) rather than Britain (geographical entity) which is leaving. Arguably, the recent trouble could have been predicted by challenging this linguistic oversight (i.e., of forgetting Northern Ireland exists).

generally left as is – Angela Merkel would never become Aingeal Uí Mhercaill. The exceptions here are royalty and the pope:

Prince Charles is **Prionsa Séarlas**.

His mam is **Banríon Eilís a Dó**.

His wife is **Beandiúc Camilla**.

Pope Francis is **Pápa Prionsias**.

Taoiseach refers specifically to the Irish prime minister* – all other PMs are **Príomh-Aire**, and **Uachtarán** is used for all presidents. A general election is **olltoghchán**. The prefix **oll**- is used when a thing is big; a giant panda, for example, is **ollphanda**. A snap election is a **toghchán tobann**. A presidential election is a **toghchán na huachtaránachta**.

While the Irish equivalent to 'home sweet home' is **níl aon tinteán mar do thinteán féin**, the 2016 homeless rights movement of the same name was left untranslated. This is consistent with how Black Lives Matter, Occupy Wall Street and other new movement names are referred to on *Nuacht* before a term is agreed – proper nouns aren't translated.

* It has also been used as the title of tribal chiefs on those occasions that such people appear on the news in Ireland.

The White House gets translated (**an Teach Bán**), but 10 Downing Street doesn't. Speaking of the colour white, another name for the bogeyman is **fear an froc bháin**, literally the man in the white overcoat.

Once upon a time, an economist was asked why so few people vote in elections. Being a good economist, he did what good economists do: patiently explained that he had actually been asked the wrong question. 'By all means ask me why 45% of people vote in referenda and 56% vote in general elections,' he said, 'or ask if and why participation in elections has dropped, but "so few"? This question assumes that a correct amount exists and that some externality or externalities are causing the actual amount to be less than the correct amount.'

Pressed on the point, he suggested that whenever you ask why so few people do anything, you should also ask why so many people don't do it. With elections, where the odds of influencing the outcome are similar to those of winning the lottery, it might make more sense for an economist to ask why people would choose to do the irrational thing, rather than the other way around.

This economist's switching of the question shares something with an expression that tech people have introduced to the mainstream: *it's a feature, not a bug*. This is the idea that something gives an unsatisfactory experience on purpose because our experience is only a side effect of the service to the actual intended user, so the service provider doesn't see your bad experience as a problem to be solved.

So when it comes to children and languages, is multilingualism a feature or a bug? Are all multilingual children products of a more successful environment than that provided by mainstream education in Ireland, or is multilingualism a transition state?

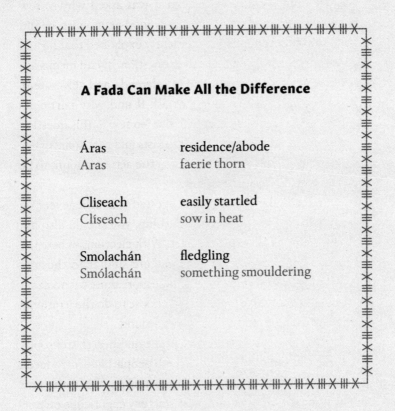

A Fada Can Make All the Difference

Áras	residence/abode
Aras	faerie thorn
Cliseach	**easily startled**
Clíseach	sow in heat
Smolachán	fledgling
Smólachán	something smouldering

MULTILINGUAL CHILDREN

Some years ago, before matrimony or parenthood had found me, I was holding the bar up at a wedding in Cork and found myself drinking next to a new father. He bore his new role with some anxiety now that the congratulatory back slaps and pints had stopped rolling in, and was beginning to fret over developmental milestones and such matters.

'Did you know, Darach, that by the age of two the formation of a person's adult personality is 90% complete?'

'I never really thought of personalities in terms of completeness, actually.'

'It's a proven fact, Darach. By the time a child is talking they're pretty much the person they're going to be for the rest of their lives. If you've made a mistake, it's set in stone.'

'Ah now, people change all the time, mate.' (This was true – I was changing from willing to unwilling participant in this conversation.)

'That's just a small amount of the other 10%. The fundamentals are everything.'

He paused and grimly drained the ends of his pint.

'What if I'm doing something wrong? Everyone thought Dr Spock* was right when we were babies, and now nobody does. What if I'm doing something that everyone thinks is the right way to do things, but it turns out to actually be really wrong?'

'I don't know, man. Maybe it comes down to the way you measure success.'

'Oh, come on. You measure success by how successful a person is. You're not one of these *but are they really happy people?*'

I was reminded of this conversation a year later when *Battle Hymn of the Tiger Mother* by Amy Chua was released. This book managed to combine eternal parental anxieties and Western geopolitical panic about rising Chinese power with a hint of old-fashioned stereotypes. In it, an American mother reflected on her Chinese–American heritage, especially the code of strictness and competitiveness to which she attributed the success of her siblings and her attempts to replicate it with her own children.

* The paediatrician, not the *Star Trek* character.

Readers around the world were horrified and thrilled to hear accounts of small children being told their home-made Mother's Day cards weren't good enough to go on the mantelpiece, marathon violin practice sessions and bans on sleepovers.

Interestingly, one of the points the book made was that Chinese mothers always took the teacher's side (not their child's) in a dispute, and decried the customer service attitude to education. This point was raised on a radio show in the context of abuse scandals in Irish schools, and my colleagues got fired up.

'No good comes from that kind of strictness. It breaks a child's spirit.'

'Sure, it's always the wildest kids who have the strictest parents.'

'Those children must be so unhappy.'

At this moment I had a terrifying thought – *what if they're not unhappy?* Or, more precisely, *what if they're no more unhappy than any other children growing up on this trashfire of a planet?* I was intrigued by how my colleagues, who never agreed on anything, were so invested in the idea that this boot camp approach to parenting was wrong. How much of this was down to their own experience of failed strictness, and how much down to their lack of faith in school results and extra-curricular excellence† creating opportunities for their kids?

A few months later, while out of town, I paid a visit to a couple expecting their first child. They were planning to move to Dublin in the next few years and considering potential schools, and were interested in picking my brain.

'You went to Gonzaga,‡ Darach. What's it like?'

'It's a good school and I had some brilliant teachers, but I think that the lads in

† Unlike in the US, the university application process in the Republic of Ireland gives no consideration to extra-curricular activities. Sports scholarships exist, but are rare and not as lucrative.

•

‡ There are three Jesuit schools in the greater Dublin area. Gonzaga is the one Joyce didn't go to.

my class would've all still ended up going to university if they'd gone somewhere else.'

The husband wasn't from the south side of Dublin but had ended up in a profession dominated by over-confident, slightly dull rugby-school chaps from that sphere. He was struck by how school ties could open doors for people, even in their forties, even in another country. He told me he'd been to school with boys who were brilliant at hurling because it was the only game in town; if they'd lived two miles up the road, they would have been brilliant at rugby instead and their world would have been very different. He had put himself under enormous pressure to gain admittance to a world that his new peers seemed to have just wandered into, and wanted to know how it worked.

'It's not getting into college itself I'm worried about really – I mean, I expect that. What's Gonzaga like for... *connections?*'

I always remember him making a mafioso gesture with his fingers when he said this, though I'm equally certain this didn't actually happen.

'Well, I've never gotten a job from a school contact, but that might just be the public sector.'

'You see, I think Gonzaga might be a good school *academically*, but... I'd be worried that if my son was really good at rugby he might never get to play for Ireland if he went there.'*

'I didn't know you were having a boy!'

* Despite racking up a truckload of chess trophies, my alma mater has never won the Leinster Senior Cup, presumably causing many talented players to be overlooked by Ireland selectors.

'We don't know yet, actually – we're not going to find out until the birth.'

The idea that he had mapped out his son's life to this level of detail before even finding out if he was a son alarmed me. The interest in a particular school – independent of an interest in education – concerned me too. I could sympathize with choosing a school with better facilities or with teachers available to teach certain subjects, but less so with seeing schools as rotary clubs or Masonic lodges.

The Irish verb **taifigh** means to analyze... not to be confused with **tafann**, to bark like a dog. I raised these conversations with my friend Simon over drinks one evening. After a promising school rugby career, he was now a psychoanalyst; his thesis (and professional speciality) was on working with young men dealing with ordinary life after the fading of teenage sporting glory.

'I never understood this whole chasing after business connections lark,' he said as he swirled a Japanese whisky under his nose. 'Successful people don't try to find connections. They endeavour to *be* connections.'

'Isn't that the same thing?'

'Wanting to have connections without wanting to be one? Wanting people to help you without wanting to help anyone yourself? It's a bit UKIP.'

(At this point we chuckled over how ridiculous the prospect of the UK ever leaving the EU was.)

'Clearly your friend is anxious about his son,' Simon continued. 'He doesn't know what the right thing to do is, but he wants to do something. In times like that – early childhood especially – spending money can release calming endorphins. And I can assure you there's always someone around to take the cash off you.'

'Then what happens?'

'Well, middle-class parenthood is all about selfishly pursuing an unfair advantage for your own kid while justifying to yourself that the rules are different for you and your family for some reason, that it's not selfish in your circumstances. The great thing about private school is that there'll always be someone who's worse than you, so you can feel better about yourself and keep telling yourself that the rules don't apply to you, because you're not as bad as *those parents*. If you must compare yourself to others, why not surround yourself with awful people?'

'When psychologists use words like selfish, narcissistic and heroic, they often mean them in different ways to the way a layperson like me would use them,' I said, 'so I'm curious to know what you mean by selfish here.'

I didn't get a straight answer, of course.

'The way we talk about things like our children's education is unhelpful. We say things are complicated when really they're just conflicted, and we call things normal when really they're aspirational. You have to make decisions with imperfect information about every single factor – the child's ability,* what the school is actually like,

---

* The context for the point about not knowing the child's ability was that at the time, many exclusive schools >>

what the other schools are actually like, what jobs will still exist in the future and so on.

'But consider this: I intend for my own son to grow up to be an honourable, self-sufficient and driven person. I want him to be exposed to as much interesting stuff as possible so that he finds something that he can get really good at. If he turns out to be the kind of guy who only wants to do the bare minimum, I want his bare minimum to be at as high a level as it possibly can be.

'Basically, I want exactly what pushy parents want, but I don't want him or my neighbours to see me as a pushy parent. I think parents, children and teachers would all be healthier if they just admitted what they want without worrying about how it made them look.'

'So do you think you'd send your son to a school like the one you went to?' I asked.

'I'm not going to get scammed like my parents were, no. The money you plan to spend on school fees, you'd be better off spending it on a nicer house in the catchment area of a great state-run school. At least you've invested your money in something that isn't going to just disappear.'

Then he added: 'There's a great *gaelscoil* near us, actually.'

It's an urgent and agonizing dilemma: how to help a

>> operated waiting lists for prospective pupils; anecdotally, some of these waiting lists were twelve years long, suggesting that parents rang the admissions office from the maternity ward.

child maximize their potential without being a tyrant. After all, being highly accomplished is deservedly a great advantage, but the damage caused by heavy-handed parenting is the stuff of legend and science.

The pressure to raise a high-performing child is something that sits very heavily on many of us with a child who has additional needs: an urge to show the world that she's as good as anyone else's kid and that she has overcome an obstacle, she has proven to the world that she is good enough... and so are we. When people try to console you after a diagnosis, they tell you about success stories they've heard, children who are involved in all sorts of activities and 'doing so well'. What happens if they don't do 'so well'?

The temptation to allow your smallie to have an innocent, carefree childhood is tempered by the thought that certain skills are much easier for young children to learn than wizened nine-year-olds or fifteen-year-old methuselahs. This is especially the case with a second language. In the Republic of Ireland, nobody disputes the value of a second or additional language, but there is sometimes a debate as to whether Irish is the best choice. So many people fail to string a sentence together after twelve or more years of learning the language.

Is this down to the intricacy of the subject itself, or to the way it's taught? After all, countries like Belgium, Switzerland and the Netherlands achieve widespread trilingualism in teenagers with similar IQs and socio-economic profiles to Irish monoglots. Should the Department of Education on Marlborough Street headhunt some Belgian headmasters to learn a thing or two?

Perhaps. There's always Survivor's Bias when discussing the bilingualism of other cultures. If you're a monoglot Anglophone, you've only spoken to foreigners who speak English and your understanding of their world is limited to the experience of people who have successfully learned English – all my German friends read *Der Spiegel* rather than *Bild*. It's also tempting to think that while English may not be empirically easier than its neighbouring European languages, there's an incentive to learn it and a wealth of films, music, books and magazines available to match a learner's specific interests.

The Belgian multilingual ideal is not without its darker side, however. As with other states with more than one language, it has a history of feuding communities compelled to live in each other's company, and still retains a Flemish zone (Flanders) and a French zone (Wallonia), with Brussels standing as a kind of no-man's land capital. And within Brussels lies Molenbeek.

This troubled and overlooked neighbourhood, a twenty-minute cycle from the European Parliament buildings, has been in the news frequently in the past few years, with various terrorist incidents in Belgium, Spain and France (including the 2004 Madrid attack and the 2015 assault on concert-goers at the Bataclan in Paris) carried out by residents or former residents of this area.

Molenbeek experiences a different variety of bilingualism than leafier parts of Brussels, one less cherished by

Belgian society. Just as other Belgian kids speak one language at home and are motivated to learn English to make themselves employable, many kids in Molenbeek speak Arabic at home and are driven to learn French or Flemish for economic reasons. There's a big difference in the way the world sees a middle-class European child speaking two or more languages and a migrant child speaking their mother tongue along with the language of their new home. One is seen as the goal of educational policy, the other as a problem to be solved.

The two best-known models for raising bilingual children are OPOL (one parent, one language) and Foreign Home (where the family language is spoken in the family home). Sometimes these methods are adopted out of necessity; sometimes they're deliberate. In the case of the latter they can often be combined with a school that teaches in the home language.

By the Power of Gaelscoil

In 2017, one of Dublin's oldest and most famous schools, Synge Street CBS, announced that it was changing. Having been an all-boys Christian Brothers school teaching in English for over 150 years, their new intake would be co-educational, and students would be educated in Irish. That a school which others already sought to emulate would make such a shift in direction set tongues wagging, and raised the topic of Irish-medium education all over again.

Ireland is obsessed with education. The value of col- 43
lege courses – based on the points required for entry, with
subjects like Medicine demanding ever more exorbitant
Leaving Cert scores – is watched like the Premiership
transfer window, and school league tables are pored over
and argued over at length. Gender wars, class conflict,
religion, county rivalries, the relative value of humanities,
trades and science, and Ireland's place in the world all
come out to play.

Inevitably these discussions converge around the inability of many people to speak Irish after eleven or twelve
years of formal Irish education, what went wrong, and
the other things children could have learned in that time.
While people lament or delight in the unpopularity of
Irish as a subject, the popularity of Irish-medium education cannot be denied. Why is this?

As with so many issues relating to the Irish language,
the story tells us a lot about Ireland itself.

─‖✕─ Schools and the Property Ladder ─‖✕─

Ireland's obsession with the education system reflects its
other obsession: the property market. When asked why
Synge Street was changing course, two factors were cited:
parent demand (of course), but also demographic changes
in the catchment area, which includes neighbourhoods of
historical significance in the Dublin 8 postcode – the Liber-
ties, Camden Street, South Circular Road and Portobello.
Since before living memory, this part of the city has been

its most multicultural (the streets behind South Circular Road were known as Little Jerusalem), as well as the home of many families employed for generations at the Guinness Brewery in St James's Gate. While it's still a diverse area, the critical change has been the impermanence of the residents. However, its proximity to the city centre makes it accessible to students from further afield.

School catchment areas are frustrating. When an area is growing rapidly there are too few schools, but when they've been built and the neighbourhood has matured, there are too few schoolchildren. This means an adult may grow up in a neighbourhood without enough schools as a teenager, but which has an attractive pupil-teacher ratio now that they've moved out – possibly into a new estate where there are no schools at all. The thought must cross their mind: What *if I just use Mam and Dad's address?*

Rathfarnham, where I grew up, was home to one of the first Gaelscoileanna – Scoil Éanna in St Enda's Park, founded by 1916 revolutionary Patrick Pearse. Even though he was an observant Catholic, he established his school to be independent from the tentacles of the Dublin archdiocese, and to this day Irish-medium schools offer parents a secular approach to education* which is increasingly popular given the repeated church scandals that have come to light over the past twenty

* Not in every instance, but frequently. Some mainstream Catholic schools offer an Irish-medium stream rather than being full Gaelscoils.

The fact that certain Irish-medium schools rank highly in those deeply problematic (Irish for problematic: **achrannach**) school league tables is clearly a factor too. Also, some parents have fair to middling Irish and want more for their kids – they see the beauty of the language, but also the doors it opens for fluent speakers, particularly in sought-after career paths like media, education, law and broadcasting. If it's one of the local schools, why not choose the Gaelscoil?

Such explanations have been found wanting by some commentators, particularly the sort with a vocal interest in the difference between the melting point of steel and the burning temperature of jet fuel. In fact, a dramatic accusation has been levelled: that the popularity of these state-funded schools is motivated by racism. The logic – if you can call it that – behind this claim is that the selection criteria for these schools (many state a preference for Irish-speaking parents) make it very hard for children from non-traditional Irish backgrounds to gain admittance.

For an accusation of this severity, surely the burden of proof is on the accuser? The difference between a theory and a conspiracy theory is always that moment when the responsibility to prove does a back flip, when a roadmap to truth is replaced with the deliberate Feng Shui of telling anecdotes, none of which prove anything on their own but which together create an atmosphere of truthiness.

The Irish for free speech is **saoirse cainte**. An audience is a **lucht éisteachta**. Having the first doesn't entitle you to the second. **Saoirse cainte** doesn't mean all opinions are **comhbhailí** (equally valid).

If the challenge to prove this accusation were taken up, demonstrating that the alleged racist factors in Gaelscoil admission policy are unique to Gaelscoileanna would be the first point to consider. I expect you'd have a hard time demonstrating that a preference for Irish-speaking parents, in those schools where such a preference is enforced, makes more of a material difference to students from minority backgrounds than priority given to siblings and children of past pupils, school fees (where they apply), the socio-economic breakdown of students repeating the Leaving Cert, and so on.

There's also the not-so-insignificant fact that plenty of students from non-traditional Irish backgrounds attend, and have attended, Gaelscoileanna.

To be a parent is to fumble from one high-stakes decision to the next while being very, very tired, and any scrap of certainty is manna from heaven. Picking a school shouldn't be an agonizing choice. In an ideal world, they'd all be great schools. But a great school can only do so much if learning isn't cherished in the home.

In their unexpected hit *Freakonomics*, Stephen Dubner and Steven Levitt present readers with a startling claim – that most parental decisions have little or no bearing on the success of a child, compared to the socio-economic situation of the parents themselves (apparently the mother's level of education is the best indicator of how far a child will go in the school system). They even make the provocative claim that once you have lots of books in your house, your child will respect books and learning – whether you yourself read them or not.

Maybe to be a parent is really to make peace with your own powerlessness; when the peer pressure and terrifying statistics come knocking, as they surely will, to be a good example to your kid and laugh them off.

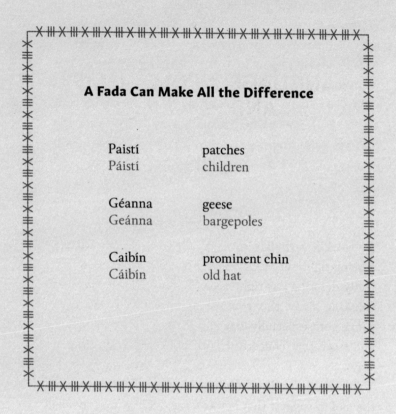

A Fada Can Make All the Difference

Paistí	patches
Páistí	children
Géanna	geese
Geánna	bargepoles
Caibín	prominent chin
Cáibín	old hat

LANGUAGE, NEOLOGISMS AND POWER

In the UK, scandals involving the state are described as being right out of Orwell; in Ireland, they're more typically described as right out of Flann O'Brien. I've been thinking about this contrast more and more since the Brexit vote, especially in regard to the assault on language and truth that concerned both writers in very different ways.

When Maeve Binchy died, a tabloid newspaper had the gall to suggest that her writing voice may have been incomplete because she never experienced motherhood. This comment was rightly condemned as ignorant, provocative and evidence of a double standard for male and female writers even after death.

However, it sat in the back of my mind and popped up at me recently. Flann O'Brien and Samuel Beckett, those masters of the very absurd and the terribly clever, never experienced the worries and joys of fatherhood. Can you still stand back, stroke your chin and take a gimlet-eyed look at the machinations of the world when you see its flaws and panic for the child you've ushered into it?

I've felt a close kinship with Flann O'Brien from the first time I dipped into a collection of his journalism. Ever since starting @theirishfor, I've felt it even more – his big break came from writing letters to the editor of the *Irish Times* (the Twitter feed of its day), which led to his getting his own column. There's his interest in languages in general and Irish in particular. There's his resistance to genres and expectations, his eloquent irreverence. And then there's his combining the life of a writer with the life of a public sector office worker. Weirdly, this is one of his biggest legacies – whenever a boy or girl in Ireland tells their parents they want to be a writer, they're advised to be sure to get a sensible day job like Flann O'Brien had.

Government work is an odd place for a writer, some would say: as well as all the stuff they've done to their citizens, governments and their administrative limbs have inflicted great suffering on language itself. Between cliquey acronyms, stuffy jargon and nauseous management lingo, sure it's a wonder we've a language left at all.

While I wouldn't go that far myself, I really do hate a lot of acronyms.

⁓⊞⊞⊞⊞⊞⊞⊞⊞⁓ OMG WMD – Acronym Hell ⁓⊞⊞⊞⊞⊞⊞⊞⊞⁓

The upper echelons of society used to use Latin terminology for aspects of their work, flaunting their importance

while excluding the Latin-less mob from their thoughts.
While this has thankfully declined, its spirit lives on – just without the Latin. Nowadays, instead of pithy Latin epithets we get graceless acronyms. While these are fine for scientific terms like inventions and diseases, appropriating the respectability of science in less honourable endeavours is bad form altogether.

They're not all evil, of course, but I dislike their presumption, their assumption that you know what they stand for and that it is well established and somehow respectable. The two most significant acronyms of the 2000s – OMG* and WMD – are both suitable examples.

* As discussed in *Motherfoclóir*, there are much earlier examples of OMG – but the 2000s was when usage spiked.

OMG is a written abbreviation that has trickled into speech, even though it has the exact same number of syllables as the term it claims to truncate, thereby saving the speaker no time at all.

WMD saves the speaker plenty of time. However, all those hours saved by not saying 'weapons of mass destruction' weren't put to use in actually finding the feckers. Shortening the term reinforced the idea that they actually existed, as real as the BBC or NHS.

The Irish for...

DIY is DFÉ (**déan féin é**).

FYI is MED (**mar eolas duit**).

LOL is GOA (**gáire os ard**).

ASAP is CLAIF (**chomh luath agus is féidir**).

DNA is ADN (**aigéad dí-ocsairibeanúicléasach**).

SME (small and medium enterprises) is GBM (**gnóthais bheaga agus mheánmhéide**).

SoMoLo (social, mobile, local) is SóMóLo (sóisialta, móibíleach, logánta). Just add fadas.

Maybe it's just me, but I find that translating acronyms subverts them a little, undermining their smugness and mocking the familiarity their claim to power rests in. It gets me thinking about the delicate relationship between writing, power and satire* in Ireland, and how the Irish language runs through it.

* *Gáire* means laugh – not to be confused with *ga aoire*, the sting of satire.

The Irish Civil Service was once described as the greatest patron of the arts since the Medicis, in that so many writers (particularly those who didn't emigrate) held day jobs there, squandering their salaries on their compulsive literary habits. The most famous is Flann O'Brien but there were flocks of others – Thomas Kinsella, Denis O'Driscoll, Richard Power, Frank O'Connor, Máirtín Ó Direáin and many more. It's hard to ride two horses at the best of times, but the business of words, which is the concern of the civil servant and of the writer, requires attitudes to language that cannot be turned on and off like a tap.

While writers who left the country could let their savage indignation off the leash, those who stayed and took the Republic's shilling were faced with a conflict of interest – could they bite the hand that fed them? Helpfully, there were regulations in place to confirm that they couldn't. In order to maintain a completely neutral civil service that could support different governments equally well, there were restrictions on political activity and publishing material that related to their work. The simplest work-around was to publish under a nom de plume.

The adjective **easurramach** is used to describe people or actions that are disrespectful, irreverent or cavalier. Flann O'Brien's cavalier attitude to his official role in his column certainly got him into hot water more than once as his writing career went from an open secret to simply open. Sadly, his novels did not find enough success in his lifetime to allow him to leave on his own terms.

Staidéar Gnó is Irish for Business Studies (Enterprise Northern Ireland didn't take my suggested slogan – 'Ulster Says Gnó' – for some reason; I presume it just didn't have that quintessence of management speak). Management speak is hard to define but easy to recognize; there's a certain pastoral quality to all that blue-tsky thinking and ducks in a row.

For example, we have deceptively bucolic-sounding entities such as the decision tree; in Irish, this is **crann cinnteoireachta** – literally a decision-making tree. Such trees are unlikely to be found in a **coilleog** (a grove, little forest or wooded area, as opposed to a **coill**, a larger forest or wooded area). **Badhbh na coille duibhe** would literally be the Badhbh of the dark (or black) forest, one of the Irish equivalents of the bogeyman.

Best practice is **dea-chleachtas**, not to be confused with **dásacht**, bravery or daring. Having said that, in Old Irish **dásacht** could also mean possessed by a demon. Conflict resolution is **réiteach coimhlinte**. There's an older term, however: **eadráin**, which doesn't have an exact match in English, refers to the act of separating fighters or quarrellers.

A flowchart is **sreabhchlár**, not to be confused with **sreabha deor**, floods of tears. Middle management is **meánbhainistíocht**, which has a lovely internal rhyme.

One of the words for errand-boy is **dioscaire**. Another is **timire** (which can also mean a travelling Irish teacher) – the devil's errand-boy is **timire an diabhail**.

Accountancy is **cuntasóireacht**. Account (be it savings or Twitter) is **cuntas**.

Céadéaga means death throes; it can also be used figuratively to refer to deep infuriation. Unrelated, I'm sure, to wage flexibility – **solúbthacht phá**.

Insider trading is **déileáil cos istigh** (trading with a foot in), which is contrary to business ethics, **eitic ghnó**. Could this apply to **gabhairín**? That means potatoes sold secretly by child dealers.

Speaking of potatoes, **spadán** doesn't have an exact match in English; *Dinneen* defines it as 'lea-land on which potatoes are sown by spreading them on the unprepared surface and covering them over with soil taken from the furrows', 'poor, fallow ground' or 'a dull, lazy, sluggish person'. Such a person might be sent to visit Human Resources, **Acmhainní Daonna**.

A **drochrud** is a bad thing, or a bad person who does bad things (**droch** meaning bad, **rud** meaning a thing). It's all so simple... unlike the word for nonfeasance, which is **neamhghníomh**. That's right – five consonants in a row! An asset-stripper is a **scamhaire sócmhainní**.

I'm sure that these nice people are just doing their jobs, suggesting wonderful efficiencies and representing their shareholders' interests. On an unrelated note, **íobartach** means victim (or subject) of a sacrifice.

The Irish for business school is **scoil ghnó**. While you're there, you might learn the difference between (perfectly legal) tax avoidance, **seachaint cánach**, as opposed to **imghabháil cánach**, (not so legal) tax evasion.* Breakdown of expenditure is **miondealú ar chaiteachas**.

* In the old days you might have paid your **cáin** (tax) with a **cianóg** (coin) or two.

Capital depreciation is **dímheas caipitil** – **dímheas** also means disrespect.

Shadow director is **scáthstiúrthóir**. On the other hand, a hunter gatherer is a **cnuasaitheoir. Logh-eineach** was an ancient tribute paid to a chief for his protection. An audit is **iniúchadh**... terrifyingly similar to **inniu**, which means today. A **creachadóir** is a raider, pillager or plunderer.

Lemon is **líomóid**. They're small, they're bitter, but I couldn't have a G & T without one. Referring to a dud car as a lemon was never very widespread in my lifetime and is utterly anachronistic now. In fact, car standards have improved so much that a lot of expressions for unreliability in motoring have become quaint and granddad-ish – jalopy, banger, even tin lizzie will have younger readers reaching for their smartphones. But what do we call a car in Irish?

+||| |||| || |||| |||- **Cars and Computers** +||| |||| || |||| |||-

Lots of us will remember the Irish word for car we learned in school – **gluaisteán**. It's a fun word to say (gloosh-tahn) and doesn't look like any related English words, so it feels authentic. Certainly better than a lame, cheesy word like **carr**, right?

Strictly speaking, **gluaisteán** means motor rather than car, and although **carr** looks and sounds like the modern English word for automobile, it predates it; it pops up in Bishop O'Brien's 1768 dictionary (meaning a cart or a spear), as well as in Middle Irish. It has an even greater claim to legitimacy, however. Both the English and Irish terms come from the Latin word *carrus*... itself a borrowing from a lost Celtic language (it originally referred to Gaulish chariots).

Much as 'text' moved from noun to verb, the word computer has moved from verb (to compute) to noun. In Old Irish, a **riomhaire** was the person in an abbey or monastery who worked out the dates of Easter and related moveable feasts; the name for this medieval computer was kept for the modern technology.

If one were to pick a new English word of the decade, the entry for the 2000s would surely be the new use of an old word, 'text' (from noun to verb) rather than a brand-new combination of syllables. For the 2010s, the word would surely be 'selfie',* a derivative of an existing word with a suffix added. But where are these English words from? In two hundred years, what origin will linguists and historians attribute to them?

I got a Nokia 3210 in 1999. It was my second ever phone and a significant upgrade from the analogue Motorola device I'd been using for the previous year, which could only hold twenty phone numbers, had no caller ID and weighed as much as a sleeping toddler. While recommending it to me, the enthusiastic saleswoman rhapsodized over battery life, memory and the concealed aerial, but didn't even mention the feature it would become known for – text messages.

SMS was an afterthought. However, these 160-character chunks of data quickly revolutionized everything from flirting to radio competitions† and were the closest product to pure profit since the selling of indulgences.

* *Féinspéisí* (a person who is very fond of themselves) is not to be confused with *féinphic*, which means a selfie.

† The once-popular expression 'answers on a postcard' now joins phrases like 'money for old rope' and 'nose to the grindstone', all relics of abandoned business practices.

I was doing my Masters at the time and was very friendly with American and Canadian classmates, and we all watched this phenomenon grip Ireland together. In 1999, they concluded that this was very much a British and Irish fad, as free local landline calls in North America made text messages much less attractive. Furthermore, over there it even cost money to receive a text, so being friends with a text message enthusiast could be an expensive vice.

Consequentially, text migrated from noun to verb in these islands before doing so across the Atlantic. Whoever first used text as a verb in print did not coin the term, but documented a trend they witnessed around them, a trend which happened on these islands first. Schoolchildren were advised not to use it as a verb in exams, until the day came that it was declared perfectly fine.

It's not my intention to make brash, nationalistic claims that Ireland 'owns' text as a verb, but rather to give some context to the process by which new uses take hold. Is the verb 'to text' Hiberno-English? Is it English-English? If it was spontaneously created in Britain and Ireland at the same time, who owns it? If it was first used in print in Ireland six weeks before the UK, does that prove anything?

A Fada Can Make All the Difference

An Albain	Scotland
An Albáin	Albania
Rósta	**roasted**
Rosta	wrist
Fúig	**leave** (form of **fág**)
Fuig	Whig (nineteenth-century liberal)

HIBERNO-ENGLISH

The Grand Language

My favourite word from *Finnegans Wake* is *sfumas-telliacinous* – hair full of pretty stars and beautiful, smoky shadows. Joyce coined it from Italian words he knew well – *stella* meaning star, *sfumato* being the smudging technique in Renaissance art used to create shadows and shade* – and possibly also *cinereo*, an elegant shade of grey (literally, ash-coloured) most commonly used in ornithology to describe plumage.

Sfumastelliacinous is a word coined by an Irish writer, but is it an Irish word? Clearly it's not in the Irish language, but can it be classed as a Hiberno-English word?

We generally take Hiberno-English to be an umbrella term for the versions of English spoken in Ireland, but there's more to it than that. The name itself is an unusual form – the choice of 'Hiberno' rather than 'Irish' as a prefix is interesting, the Latin form declaring a certain serious-ness of intent. Yet much writing on Hiberno-English has focused on its slang character, its quirks and its whimsical flourishes.

Although there are a handful of glossaries, such as Terry Dolan's excellent *Dictionary of Hiberno-English*, these focus on local linguistic peculiarities and are intended to be used alongside a conventional dictionary. Other Anglosphere countries like the US, Australia and Canada have their own dictionaries which reflect their use of the language, but there's no official dictionary of Hiberno-English. Does this hamper serious academic work in both languages here?

After Brexit, the Republic of Ireland will be the largest state in the European Union with English as an official lan-guage. If English, as the most common second language, continues to be the working language of the EU, will that working language be Hiberno-English? If your first thought upon hearing that question is 'no, of course not', it's worth considering why, and what this says about the English of Ireland and the English of the EU.

First, Euro-speak is widely and correctly seen as a ghastly Frankenstein's monster, a compromise that makes nobody happy – all those acronyms, Germanic capitaliz-ation and long sentences. Consider this stirring extract from the Lisbon Treaty:

'The cross-references to the articles, sections, chapters, titles and parts of the Treaty on European Union and of the Treaty on the Functioning of the European Union, as well as between them, shall be adapted pursuant to paragraph 1 and the references to paragraphs of the said articles as renumbered or re-ordered by the provisions of this Treaty shall be adapted in accordance with those provisions. References to the articles, sections, chapters, titles and parts of the Treaty on European Union and of the Treaty establishing the European Community contained in the other treaties and acts of primary legislation on which the Union is founded shall be adapted pursuant to paragraph 1 of this Article. References to recitals of the Treaty on European Union or to paragraphs or articles of the Treaty on European Union or of the Treaty establishing the European Community as renumbered or re-arranged by the provisions of this Treaty shall be adapted pursuant to this latter. Such adaptations shall, where necessary, also apply in the event that the provision in question has been repealed.'*

People don't speak to each other like this; the EU habit of writing documents that only make sense if you've read the documents they refer to *and* the documents that those referred documents themselves refer to is like a high modernist novel.

* Article 5.2,
Final Provisions
Lisbon Treaty

Is this hyper-formality the opposite of slang, or just the slang of a particular group? This paragraph arguably doesn't count as jargon, as none of the individual words are beyond the vocabulary of a typical Junior Cert student. It's more that a manner of speech has been established that is known to other users, and that familiar words have a precise meaning in that context. Just like Hiberno-English.

The mainstream view of Hiberno-English is that the vernacular in Ireland is a layer of English paint over a lumpy Gaelic undercoat, with the distinctive features of English here attributed to the Irish under the surface. This is based on the notion of Irish speakers learning English vocabulary and stringing sentences together with Irish syntax, using Irish words where their English vocabulary fails.

While this is true up to a point and a useful guideline in general, it does no harm to delve a little bit further into the distinctive traits of Hiberno-English, beyond quirky slang, and ask if the stimuli that made it unique still apply. Is English in Ireland still influenced by Irish or earlier forms of Hiberno-English? Is there a Hiberno-Irish that's influenced by Hiberno-English? As with the stages of Old, Middle, Early Modern and Modern English, do we have stages of Hiberno-English?

Undercoat theory doesn't explain how some globally used English words have a different use here. Here are some examples for your consideration. Each word has a particular use in Ireland, but can't necessarily be directly connected to a root in Irish.

ʏʏʏʏʏʏʏ Craic ʏʏʏʏʏʏʏ

Let's start with the most famous Hiberno-English word of all, which is also a word of contested origin. **Craic** means fun, particularly in a stereotypically Irish context, and has been accepted as such for over a quarter of a century.

However, some people get hot under the collar at the idea that it and other Hiberno-English words are not authentically Irish, whereas others get extremely protective of their local origin.

The case for this word having an Irish origin comes from an entry in the 1977 *Foclóir* (meaning conversation or chat) and its similarity to **craiceáilte** (mad) and **ag bualaidh craicinn** (having sex*). While it's not found in earlier dictionaries, omission is not proof that it wasn't in use.

The case against **craic** being an Irish word hinges on the spelling – specifically, that the word was widely spelled 'crack' before the early '90s and that the -aic ending is as inauthentic as the umlauts on Mötley Crüe. Anti-craic types cite the original record inlay for the Christy Moore song 'The Crack Was Ninety in the Isle of Man' and the existence of a Middle English word *crack* with similar meaning. They add that this word has many meanings (over fifty on dictionary.com), with some related to having fun: wisecrack, crack a joke, crack up laughing.

* If you've never heard this expression before you might be due some *gnéasoideachas* – sex education.

So who's right? The question cuts right to the heart of our understanding of what Hiberno-English is and isn't:

- Does an English word have to be confined to Ireland to be Hiberno?

- Does an English word have to come from the Irish language to be Hiberno?

- Can a 'normal' English word have particular Hiberno-English usages?

- Can a 'normal' English word have a particular spelling in Ireland for its Irish contexts?

- Is Hiberno-English now closed to new words?

⅄ Irish Origin v. Global Word, Local Use ⅄

Let's humour the anti-*craic* brigade for a moment and park (not necessarily abandon) the idea that it comes from the Gaeilge. Would this be a killer blow? What if we could establish a sincerely earned place in Hiberno-English for *craic* that followed other rules for English as spoken in Ireland?

Let's start by pointing out that Hiberno-English is not limited to loanwords from Irish. Consider 'grand'.

⅄⅄⅄⅄⅄⅄ Grand ⅄⅄⅄⅄⅄⅄

Comedian Ed Byrne once remarked that if the Grand Canyon was in Ireland, it'd be called the Fuckin' Deadly Canyon. At some point in language, the Irish use of 'grand' became less emphatic than elsewhere. Readers of *The Catcher in the Rye* might remember Holden Caulfield's distaste for the word:

> 'Grand. There's a word I really hate. It's phony. I could puke every time I hear it.'

While J. D. Salinger does attribute a diluted Irish heritage to his most famous character,* Holden isn't using it in the Irish sense here. *Catcher* came out in 1951, twenty-nine years after *Ulysses*. Consider Joyce's usage:

> – *Grand is no name for it, said Buck Mulligan. Wonderful entirely. Fill us out some more tea, Kinch. Would you like a cup, ma'am?*

And later on:

> – *Milly has a position down in Mullingar, you know.*
> – *Go away! Isn't that grand for her?*
> – *Yes. In a photographer's there. Getting on like a house on fire.*

This use (satisfactory, but short of wonderful) would equate to **togha** or **go breá** in Irish, but these terms don't owe anything to 'grand'.

---

* The fact that Holden's two signature words, 'grand' and 'phony', both have an Irish angle in their etymology is a remarkable coincidence. 'Phony' is thought to come from *fáinne* (ring), in reference to fake jewellery sold at fairs in the early twentieth century.

ᛣᛣᛣᛣᛣᛣ **Article** ᛣᛣᛣᛣᛣᛣ

Describing someone attractive, troublesome or both as 'quite an article' is listed in *The Dictionary of American Slang*, but it's fair to say this is not a current or widespread use stateside. However, calling someone 'a right article' (a piece of work, a bit dangerous) is still popular in Ireland, so much so that the foclóir.ie entry lists this usage in third place, ahead of 'section of a legal document' and 'article of faith'.

This is an instance of a particular meaning not being unique to Ireland but being far more prevalent here. Another example would be a Limerick person addressing a third party as 'kid', regardless of their age: not the only place that this happens by any stretch of the imagination, but too widespread to not be recognized as a local feature.

ᚋᚋᚋᚋᚋᚋᚋ **After** ᚋᚋᚋᚋᚋᚋᚋ

Sometimes we use language in a deliberate way, and sometimes we blurt things out without thinking, such as in a moment of scalding pain. While an English person might declare (after uttering the relevant expletives) 'I scalded myself', it's more typical in Ireland to hear 'I'm after scalding myself'. In less dramatic situations, you might hear someone say 'I'm after ringing her' as opposed to the classic 'I rang her'.

Much has been made of the prevalence of the passive voice in the Irish language (**tá uaigneas orm** – 'It is sadness on me' – rather than 'I am sad'), and from this armchair psychologists have drawn conclusions about the national disposition: that we are a passive and fatalistic people.

Both **tá uaigneas orm** and 'I am sad' have three words. In English: pronoun, verb, adjective. In Irish: verb, adjective, prepositional pronoun. Irish uses prepositional pronouns

(*orm, ort, air, uirthi*) and English doesn't, usually expressing
these ideas with the combination of a preposition (on) and
a pronoun (me). The inclusion of a preposition such as 'after'
in a Hiberno sentence, where not called for in English-
English, is a borrowing from Irish.

⅄⅄⅄⅄⅄⅄⅄ **Now/Sure** ⅄⅄⅄⅄⅄⅄⅄

These words are used in Ireland in the same way as every-
where else, but they also have an additional function as
interjections, as a kind of spoken punctuation. While this
isn't unique to Ireland, it is a flourish that a person imitating or exaggerating an Irish accent might use. Although
nobody says 'to be sure, to be sure' in real life, there are
occurrences of 'sure' being detached from only meaning
certainty.

Consider the richly ironic praise given to a day's fine
weather: 'Sure, where else would you get it?' It's hard to
explain (especially to an English sub-editor) how this sentence doesn't really work without the 'sure'. I'd stick my
neck out and say that sometimes people use 'sure' as a pre-
cursor to a sentence where the content is far from sure and
some degree of irony is expected.

The word 'now' is used in non-temporal contexts in Ireland, particularly at the end of a sentence. Sometimes this
is a friendly touch: 'There you go, now' might be spoken
by a shopkeeper concluding a transaction, as opposed
to the undressed 'There you go'. But it can also be defiant
in the face of a threat or ultimatum:

– Eoin said he's going to bate you after school.
– Oh, will he, now?

The Hiberno 'now' has been compared to those helpful yet inscrutable words *bitte* in German and *prego* in Italian, which morph into the required context like a toggle button in electronics whose effect is determined from the context of the current state.

The Irish for 'now' is **anois** and the Irish for 'sure' is **cinnte**. There's some incidence of these words being used in Irish in the ways flaunted above – **imigh leat anois** would mean 'run along now' rather than leave immediately.

ϓϓϓϓϓϓϓ Lads ϓϓϓϓϓϓ

The non-gender-specific use of 'lads', thought to have originated in the Midlands, is fairly widespread in Ireland.

ϓϓϓϓϓϓϓ Himself ϓϓϓϓϓϓ

This exists in mainstream English as the reflexive and the emphatic appositive form of the masculine third person singular. In layman's terms, if the chap is being tagged twice in the sentence this form comes into play: he bit himself, he said it himself, he has only himself to blame.

The use of 'himself' outside this context, especially as a nickname or a title, is common in Ireland. Given that it exists in Scotland too, we might consider whether this word, while not coming from Irish, might pair up with a pan-Gaelic usage.

The relevant term in Irish here is **féin** – **mé féin** (myself), **sé féin** or **é féin** (himself) and, of course, **sinn féin** (ourselves). That last one is one of the best-known Irish terms because of the famous political party, which is often translated as 'Ourselves Alone'* rather than just 'ourselves', which gives a clue to how the Irish term (in two parts) doesn't exactly match the English term (one part).

---

* In Robert MacLiam Wilson's satirical 1990s novel *Eureka Street*, global attention is turned to Northern Irish politics, in particular the Just Us party.

⅄⅄⅄⅄⅄⅄⅄ (Make A) Show ⅄⅄⅄⅄⅄⅄⅄

Some international dictionaries state that to 'make a show' means to be ostentatious – to make a show of being nice to someone, and so forth. However, to make a show of someone in Ireland – especially a holy show – is to make a spectacle of them, to embarrass and shame them. This is consistent with the Irish-language usage – **rinne sé seó do féin**, he made a show of himself.

⅄⅄⅄ Global Word, Local Spelling ⅄⅄⅄

A contestant on American gameshow *Jeopardy* received widespread sympathy in 2017 after having one of his responses declared wrong. Asked about the theme tune to gritty '90s high school drama *Dangerous Minds*, he came up with 'Gangster's Paradise' instead of the correct answer, 'Gangsta's Paradise'. His defenders furiously claimed that these two words are pretty much the same.

But are they?

While 'gangsta' clearly emerged from 'gangster', the significance in switching the -er to an -a is critical, transporting the violent, suitably networked criminal from the world of James Cagney movies to the land of NWA lyrics and other hip-hop and rap.

Sometimes a word has multiple meanings in multiple contexts, but a derivative form only carries one of those meanings with it. Consider 'gal' as a derivative of girl. Now there are some circumstances in which it might be appropriate to refer to a twenty-eight-year-old chartered accountant as a girl (when she is socializing with her female peers, for example), but plenty of others in which it is not (the workplace).

While 'gal' carries this informal use for female peers of any age, it doesn't carry the other meanings – you wouldn't ask a new grandparent if their grandchild was a boy or a gal. So it goes with fella/fellow (you won't be appointed a fella of the university) and so on. These derivative forms phonetically follow how these words were pronounced in the specific, informal contexts in which they were used and widely heard around the world – old American movies.

Such derivative forms are a part of Hiberno-English too, and while their origin owes nothing to the Irish language, they often find their way into normal speech here.

The above process is a clue as to how Catholics have avoided Ireland's stubbornly unrepealed (if rarely enforced) blasphemy laws. While uttering the name of Jesus in a non-prayerful context could be seen as taking the Lord's name in vain, the familiar form 'Jaysus' (see also Jayziz, Jeeeee-azus and so on) is clearly a different word, entitled to a separate dictionary entry. Jaysus is used all over the Republic (less so over the border) but is particularly associated with Dublin, where its function in speech is closer to seasoning than flavour.

Continuing on a religious theme, we have 'Prod' – not to be confused with the farm machinery that dispenses electric shocks to cattle. While this has been used as an insult, there's also a tradition of people self-identifying with the term, usually irreverently.

The derivative term Prod, with its prominent final D, emerged from Protestant, a word with no letter D. The way Protestant is pronounced in Ireland softens that first T and marks the familiar form as particular to Ireland. This softening process disconnects Prod from the 'protest' root word.

In case you were wondering, the Irish words for consubstantiation and transubstantiation are **comhshubstaintiú** and **tras-substaintiú**.

ҮҮҮҮҮҮҮ **Eejit** ҮҮҮҮҮҮҮ

While the first T in Protestant is pronounced as a D in Irish spoken English, the D in idiot presents as a J. Eejit is definitely a softer reprimand than idiot; it's worth mentioning that at a less sensitive point in history, idiot was a technical term used by qualified medical practitioners. This is why you might call a friend's child an eejit, but not get away with calling them an idiot. Eejit is innocent of such a history – if one were to translate the great Russian novel into English, one would not use *The Eejit* as the title, even for an Ireland-only release.

ҮҮҮҮҮҮҮ **Feck/Shite** ҮҮҮҮҮҮҮ

Same drill here. Just as an oil painter has pure blue on her palette and mixes it with tiny amounts of white or yellow to get the exact right shade for the morning sky or the treacherous sea, so do Irish people use feck in some circumstances and fuck in others. While shit and shite can both refer to excrement and the processes involved, nobody ever refers to coitus as fecking or a feck. It's a derivative of the expletive only.

ҮҮҮҮҮҮҮ **Langer** ҮҮҮҮҮҮҮ

A pattern has been identified for slang words that mean both a penis and an idiot, such as the Yiddish *schmuck* and the Cork langer. It starts with an object that looks like a

penis (banana, sausage) being used as a euphemism for the
membrum virile. Once it catches on and is widely established, it starts to be used to refer to people who are either
foolish, obnoxious or both. There aren't any examples of a
word starting off as meaning a fool or an obnoxious person
and graduating to mean a penis; it's one-way traffic. However the original source of langer is unclear, and conflicting
theories abound, such as:

1. It comes from **longar**, an Irish word describing the act of
   swinging from side to side;

2. It comes from **long**, a ship or container vessel. This is
   plausible in the context of Cork City's proud maritime
   history;

3. It was coined at the expense of the golf legend Bernhard
   Langer, possibly by a Corconian who had a gambling
   loss. While this may have magnified its use, it seems like
   a stretch to think he started the whole thing;

4. A popular theory is that when the Royal Munster
   Fusiliers were stationed in India, they were frequently
   bothered by langur monkeys (who are annoying and
   have long tails), who would interfere with their equip-
   ment and make shows of themselves. There's a long
   history of neologisms with definite military origins
   (pyjamas, pukka, the bee's knees), partly on account of
   the exact start dates involved and shared experiences,
   but also because of the wealth of correspondence from
   confirmed participants which allows comparisons

to be made – soldiers write letters and their families keep them for a long time. It's important to clarify that having a wealth of words with military origins does not increase the probability that a word of doubtful progeny is likely to be a military one;

5. Some langer just made it up.

Perhaps when we finally settle this one we might also clarify the origins of the nickname gooch in Munster, typically awarded to an awkward red-haired boy. The fact that this is slang for the perineum in America doesn't seem to have lessened its popularity.

ɎɎɎɎɎɎ **Local Flavour** ɎɎɎɎɎɎ

Some words only appear to have an Irish meaning to Irish people. To the rest of the world they just appear to be normal English nouns.

ɎɎɎɎɎɎ **Road frontage** ɎɎɎɎɎɎ

In Dinneen's foclóir, a **comhla breac** is a magical trapdoor to fairy dwellings hidden among rocks. The Irish obsession with property, right down to where entrances are placed, can be found in both folklore and planning laws. At its most literal, road frontage just means land adjacent to a road. So far, so boring. However, agricultural land with proximity to a main road is more likely to be approved by planning authorities for residential use. Some councils restrict the number of one-off houses along a road (say, five per quarter kilometre) for environmental and infrastructural reasons, so the more road frontage one has, the less likely one is to be turned down when applying for planning permission for that massive dream home.

This has led to road frontage becoming a kind of synecdoche for a new partner's overall prospects or eligibility – *Does s/he have road frontage?* Like all true slang, its power rests in the fact that only 'people like you' know what it means.

A **scim** can mean a film or fine covering, such as that which seals the eyelids while we sleep. A **scim dhraíochta** is a magical haze or film on favoured farmland, typically denoting prosperity. On the opposite end of the spectrum, a **pailitéir** is a fella without any land. In particular, a **pailitéir** is a farmer who holds conacre (**conacra**), a system of renting farmland unfavourable to the tenant.

⅄⅄⅄ Cans weather / Big bag of cans ⅄⅄⅄ (with the lads)

Ireland has a storied relationship with sunlight and rain; the Romans had been to Scotland but still called Ireland Hibernia (land of winter). This can lead to a panicked fear of missing out when a spell of unexpected good weather commences. So far, so indistinguishable from England or Sweden.

However, to declare good weather to be cans weather is a state of mind – all those plans to meet friends that kept getting postponed are suddenly expedited, you work twice as hard and twice as fast so you can finish up early, you eschew the packed bars and their cursed round systems for the comforts of nature. Then you arrive to meet your friends, each one of you bringing a big bag of cans of beer or cider. At some point in the last three years, 'big bag of cans' became the cellar door* of Hiberno-English, a delightful combination of syllables to say and hear – and in Irish too, where it's **mála mór cannaí**. We generally don't translate brand names, but doesn't the literal Irish for Dutch Gold, **Ór Ollannach**, sound lovely?

---

* Cellar door was declared by Tolkien to be the most beautiful sequence of syllables in English.

⅄⅄⅄ Bailout / Quantitative easing / ⅄⅄⅄ Frontloading / PIGS

I'm not trying to be smart here, but the absence of a Hiberno-English dictionary is very sorely felt in relation to the financial, economic and sociological vocabulary of the evening news. While a normal English dictionary will include entries for these terms, it's unlikely that the particular Irish context of their use will be flagged.

In the last years of the 2000s, these terms were in the news every day and if you weren't paying attention upon their earliest utterance, it was hard to keep up. A student in the 2030s doomed to write a thesis on this critical period

of Irish history will only get part of the story if they look
these terms up, as if, when looking up Watergate, the defi-
nition only mentioned the hotel and a type of gate.

For example, 'quantitative easing' in dictionary.com is
'the policy by which a central bank creates money and
uses it to purchase financial assets, thereby increasing the
money supply and stimulating a weak economy'. This is
not untrue, and sounds fairly polite.

In the case of recent Irish history, however, the central
bank in question was in Frankfurt and the weak economy
in question was in Ireland, which had other economies
bound to it through the machinery of the European Union.
So quantitative easing referred to debate about whether
or not the European Central Bank should perform actions
that affected all of the Eurozone for Ireland's sake, and
whether the consequences would be worse if they didn't.

Bank bailouts have happened in lots of places lots of
times, but The Bailout in Ireland was a moment of hubris
and despair, leaving people openly questioning whether
we should have ever gone to the bother of becoming an
independent country at all. A lot of the commentary on
Ireland's economic crash in the global media reflected on
the excesses of the Celtic Tiger, and a hangover was used
as an analogy on more than one occasion. The financial
hardship was bad enough, but now we had been made a
show of.

I can't speak for Greece and Portugal, but I suspect they
didn't question their nation's right to exist as a consequence
of a global financial crisis. I mention these two countries

in particular because the acronym PIGS (or PIIGS)* was used in the British media a lot around this time as a catch-all phrase for the delinquent economies of the Eurozone. A future reader, without the aid of a Hiberno-English dictionary, might miss out on this subtlety.

* In the rough and tumble of the financial crisis that led to the arrival of the IMF, there was some debate as to whether the I in PIGS meant all or some of Iceland, Ireland and Italy.

⅄⅄⅄⅄⅄ Cóála agus cangarú ⅄⅄⅄⅄⅄

The Irish for boomerang is **búmarang**... not to be confused with **búm** (boom) or **rang** (a class, in the educational sense). Speaking of **rang**, could the Australians teach us a thing or two? Whenever an Irish-language origin is attributed to an Irish word (like **craic**), there's a weird amount of scepticism and a perverse glee if a different root meaning is established. Currently, the Oxford English Dictionary notes in the entry for 'deadly' that using this term to denote something wonderful is 'Irish and Australian usage'. If our Antipodean mates have their own English dictionary and we don't, there'll be more evidence to support an Australian origin to this phrase as the years go by, widely in use in Dublin in the eighties when migration traffic was entirely one way.

When we think of Australian English, we tend to think of 'g'day' and 'strewth' and such pleasantries that:

- fit in with our perception of that country, particularly as being informal, outgoing, full of surprises;

- are distinct to that country ('chunder'); and

- have a well-known source such as an Australian film, advertisement or TV show – the famously inauthentic 'shrimps on the barbie' being the classic example.

When an Australian word goes mainstream and becomes more famous than its source, is it still Australian? A case in point is 'selfie'. The *Macquarie Dictionary* – the foremost authority on Australian English – claims that it's consistent with well-documented Aussie slang patterns: 'sickie' for sick day, 'mozzie' for mosquito, 'sunnies' for sunglasses and 'kindie' for kindergarten. It also says the first recorded use of selfie was in Australia (on an ABC Science – Australian Broadcasting Corporation – message board in 2002). Furthermore, *Macquarie* also identifies 'toddler' as an English word of Australian origin. Does this make it Australian English? If so, how should that govern its use?

Perhaps even more than the undercoat of Irish, the single most notable characteristic of Hiberno-English is the lack of a dictionary. Australian, Canadian, New Zealand and American forms of English all have local chapters of Collins, as well as dictionaries of their own, but Ireland does not. This has indulged the perception that Hiberno-English is a slang or even a creole, rather than the stuff of business communiqués and university lectures. It has hampered research and debate in the field, giving undue weight to anecdote. Critically, its absence has been a loss to research in Irish.

Rather than expecting the Irish usage of English to be recorded correctly elsewhere and sulking when this doesn't happen, we should realize that it's essential that a dictionary of Hiberno-English be undertaken or an Irish edition of one of the major English dictionaries be released. This information is also vitally important for machine learning technologies as automated services become more and more important.

One of my all-time favourite pieces of writing about language is a short story (although whether it's actually a story is debatable), 'Uncleftish Beholding' by Poul Anderson. The author takes a simple concept – what if the English language had no Greek or Latin loanwords at all – and tries to explain how simple atomic chemistry would be described in that world. This calls for a newly-imagined vocabulary which gives an insight into how the scientific words we use were created.

For example, elements (the simplest chemical substances) are called *firststuffs*. Hydrogen is named *waterstuff* and oxygen is named *sourstuff*, following their literal meanings. Uranium is called *Ymirstuff*, as he chooses the equivalent Norse God to Uranus. An atom is an *uncleft* as it cannot be split (or can it?), and the word 'theory' (on account of its Greek root connecting it to theatre and different people coming together to understand an idea) is interpreted as *beholding*. As you read 'Uncleftish Beholding' and get used to its internal logic, you start to notice jarringly familiar words like iron, tin and lead, elements well enough known to speakers of Old English to have non-Latin names.

The appearance of these recognizable faces in an uncanny crowd of slightly-off strangers makes a point about the shared history of science and language. Some elements have been around since before the written word, and their old names have resisted later loanwords. The discovery of certain more volatile elements happened at a time when the classical languages were a shared green space that facilitated the will to learn and promulgate knowledge, to ennoble the scientific spirit. Later twentieth-century scientific terminology reflects American hegemony, especially with the growth of the Internet just after the Cold War.

Chemistry and physics terminology in Irish often follows the English-language term closely – **hidrigin** for hydrogen, **ocsaigin** for oxygen – and this is sometimes sniffed at, as if it reflects poorly on Irish scientific traditions and achievements. However, these words follow their Latin forms in most European languages (*hidrogenoa* and *oxigenoa* in Basque, *hydrogène* and *oxygène* in French), including English. Furthermore, those elements and scientific phenomena known to Irish farmers and fishermen have native names: The Irish word for phosphorescence is the short and snappy **bairís**. That's just the general term, though; there are others. For example, **tine thanaidhe** is defined by

Dinneen as a phosphorescent light on the teats and udder of a cow in wet weather. This is completely different of course from **tine ghealáin**, defined as a light emitted from putrid fish or rotten wood, or the luminous track of a ship or boat in summer through the sea. On the topic of fish and not wanting to exclude zoological terminology from our scientific discussion, *Dinneen* defines a **scudal** as 'a useless fish... said to be the ugliest fish in existence'. Still not as bad as what they said about him.

While there might not be many chemistry labs conducting their business *as Gaeilge*, there are other areas of scientific endeavour where the Irish language is asserting itself. In fact, information technology has created unprecedented opportunities for Irish speakers to connect with each other.

COMPUTER LANGUAGES
AND IRISH

In the 1980s there was an ad for a computer with the tagline 'So easy an adult can use it'. This went unchallenged; adults are regularly astonished at how intuitively children can use technology that they themselves struggle hopelessly to learn. Is this because children are smarter, or just that they never got used to the system the technology replaced?

When I was in school in the nineties, my classmates and I were encouraged by parents and teachers to 'do computers'. They themselves weren't entirely sure what doing computers was exactly, but there was apparently a lot of money in it. A friend of mine had a Commodore 64 (his father did computers) and we played games on it. Our teachers and parents didn't consider this to be doing computers; it was something far less worthwhile. Games were expensive, addictive, hurt the eyes, melted the brain and jacked up the electricity bill.

While the world of computer technology was known to be highly lucrative and these machines were coming to replace many kinds of jobs, computer games were treated with suspicion – closer to pinball machines than chess sets.* If only there was a way to encourage children to get comfortable with computers without playing games or having fun, our elders thought.

They meant well, of course, but they didn't consider the multiple options within doing computers – the hardware, the software, the graphics, the programming, the various kinds of code – and didn't allow for the fact that these things would all start to make sense to a young adult in the context of talking about games with other gamers.

* The Irish for chess, **ficheall**, translates literally as wood intelligence (referring to the wooden pieces).

Why won't this game work on my computer? *Memory. It's a different make. You need a patch.*

Those concepts are meaningless until they're stopping you from making a blue hedgehog collect magic coins, but they become urgent in your pursuit of a pastime. Children love to learn but hate to pay attention, and all my friends who studied Computer Science at university first became interested when they were thrilled by a video game and wondered how it worked.

A computer game can be either a **físchluiche** (video game) or a **cluiche ríomhaire** (computer game). The terminology for computer gaming in Irish reflects the highs and lows of translation practice.

A gamer is a **cluichire**; a two-player game is a **cluiche**
beirte. I'm certain that plenty of GAA enthusiasts balk at
the idea of the same word, **cluiche**, being used for playing a
hurling match outdoors on a cold early Saturday morning
as for playing an Xbox game indoors on a warm Tuesday
afternoon. Yet here we are.

A checkpoint save is the quite literal **sábháil ag seicphointe**. **Seicphointe** is the word used for Garda checkpoints
too; the concept of stopping people on a road to make sure
they were behaving themselves didn't exist in Old Ireland
(it might have made the *Táin* a good bit shorter).

Some gaming neologisms are compounds of existing
forms.

Freemium is **saorimirt** (free play).

One-handed gameplay is **imirt leathláimhe**. As **leath**
means half, one-handed literally means half of a pair of
hands here.

A sidequest is a **seachthóraíocht**. Some readers will recognize the word **tóraíocht** in there, meaning pursuit (such
as that of doomed lovers Diarmuid and Gráinne).

A cut scene is a **preabradharc** – **radharc** (vision, scene,
the name of a documentary series on RTÉ in the eighties)
+ **preab** (jump, bounce, start).

Instant replay is **athfhéachaint** – the same term used in
sports broadcasting.

Open world game is **cluiche fánaíochta** – literally
wandering game. Non-player character is **carachtar
ríomhrialaithe**. The prefix **ríomh-** is used for works that refer
to the world of computers, so the neologism **ríomhrialaithe**

means computer-controlled. Sure, maybe it could refer to the lot of us, so?

Platform game is **cluiche ardán**. An **ardán** is a small height or level; you might also recognize it from bilingual signage, meaning terrace. To level up in a game is **leibhéal a ardú**. A high score is an **ardscór**. An easy way to remember this one is that it's an 'ard score to beat.

Gamer language and terminology formation tends to consist of either acronyms for unwieldy descriptions (MMORPG, massive multiplayer online roleplaying game) or slang words for the shared experiences of gamers (pwned, based on a celebrated attempt by a victorious gamer to gloatingly type 'owned' at his defeated rival).

If you don't like the English word pwned, you certainly won't care for the Irish translation, **pwnáil**. You might prefer the translation of nerf, a term referring to a game being updated to make it more challenging, usually by making weapons weaker – this is just **lagú**, a pre-existing word for 'weakening'.

A cheat, in the context of gaming only, is an **aicearra**, the general term for a short cut. This sounds intriguingly like the Japanese name Akira. A cheat in cards, business or love would be a **séitéir**, **caimiléir** or **feallaire**.

Button mash is **scaollbhrúigh cnaipí**, literally the pan-icked pressing of buttons. As well as meaning buttons on clothing, keyboards or control devices, **cnaipe** has other meanings. The derivative **cnaipín** – specifically **cnaipín sicín** – is used to mean chicken nugget. Just in case you like to play Xbox and eat nuggets at the same time.

ollchluiche rólimeartha ilimreoirí ar líne. ORIAL, then? A turn-based strategy (TBS) game is **cluiche straitéise sealaíochta**. Making a new acronym out of this one would lead to confusion with the computer language CSS, so it might be best left be.

Finally, a zero-sum game (where one player can only progress at the expense of another) is **cluiche suime nialais**. Zero-sum thinking has become all too widespread in the Trump era, but there was plenty of it before too. The idea that learning and having fun cannot coexist has not been helpful; nor has the idea that an interest in something beautiful and challenging, like the Irish language, takes up space in the brain that could be used for something more lucrative.

The Irish for cod is **trosc**, but you could be forgiven for mistakenly thinking it's **cód**, which actually means code. Language changes, and parents, teachers and politicians would never be so ridiculously backward as to speak of doing computers anymore. Instead they talk about coding. Just as Dustin Hoffman's character in *The Graduate* once received the immortal one-word career advice 'plastics', modern students often just get 'coding'.

It was serendipitous that the Celtic Tiger happened at the same time as the rise of the first wave of Internet businesses, and that many of those businesses set up in Dublin. There was polite confusion about what they actually did and how they made money from it. One thing they did, however, was coding, which was very easy if you learned it young. Some even suggested that coding be taught in school instead of Irish.

——✕⫴✕⫴✕—— Computer Languages ——✕⫴✕⫴✕——

An infinite loop is a **lúb éigríochta**. As well as meaning loop, **lúb** can mean deceit. No doubt you've found yourself trapped in a seemingly infinite loop at work, and you wished that you could just tell your machine to go and shite. Apple co-founder Steve Wozniak once said, 'Never trust a computer you can't throw out a window,' but the little ones aren't much better. If only we could speak to them.

Hypertext Markup Language, commonly known as HTML, is one of the simplest computer languages to learn. It's composed of instructions contained within angle-bracketed terms, such as:

```
<html>all the code goes between these two</html>
<head>some text here</head>
<title>Craic Baby</title>
```

It's easy enough for a non-techie to get their head around the concept of a tag within a pair of angle-brackets. The real fun begins when there are brackets within brackets within brackets...

When I was learning HTML, I found myself referring to the backslash in the second bracket as the **séimhiú**, as

though it was the genitive version of the term in the first
bracket. Strange as it may seem, this helped me remember it.

The rise of computers happened in the post-war era, a time linguistically unlike other periods of scientific advancement. All the top scientific journals were published in English, and more research funding than ever was funnelled through American universities. The prevalence of English was part of the background of key developments in computing, and had an influence in ways that didn't occur to the protagonists at the time, especially in the creation of computer languages.

According to the HOPL (History of Programming Languages) database, there are over 8,500 programming languages on record (each one unforgivingly literal in its interpretation of your instructions); roughly 3,200 of these originated in the US, the UK or another English-speaking jurisdiction. Inevitably, this includes languages developed by people with English as a second language. Of the other two thirds of computer languages, many that were created outside the Anglosphere (Python from the Netherlands, for example) are still based on English syntax.

You can see this if you view the HTML of a German- or French-language website and see that it is written in English. One consequence is that mainstream computer languages like HTML are typically restricted to unaccented letters. This affects our German friend ß, our Spanish buddy ñ and our Norwegian pal ø, as well as the five vowels with fadas in Irish (and their identical matches in French).

I mentioned earlier that texting as a cultural phenom-enon caught on early in Ireland. What I did not mention was that for much of the 2000s, mobile phone service pro-viders in Ireland were charging people extra to text in Irish on the grounds that á, é, í, ó and ú used up more data than the unaccented twenty-six letters. Particularly galling was the fact that Spanish, French and Turkish mobile phone companies (sometimes part of the same multinational as the Irish one) were using the same technology but didn't see this as a problem; even if they did, government regu-lators in those countries didn't allow them to charge extra for these characters. While this problem has since been resolved and effectively made redundant by free mes-saging apps, the reluctance to challenge it left a bad taste for many.

The impression that the Irish language is incompatible with computer technology – or that it's somewhat com-patible but a bloody nuisance – is one that needs to be put to bed forever. As part of recording the *Motherfoclóir* pod-cast series, I met with Neal Ó Riain, a data scientist living in London who created a basic computer language based on Irish called Áireamhán (Irish for calculator). While Ó Riain is modest about the capacities of Áireamhán, the fact remains that it works within its own terms – it has the quality of completeness that all computer languages need – and it can inspire other people to do more.

The invention of the typewriter (not to mention the training and manufacturing costs) was a factor in the adoption of modern lettering in Irish; it remains to be seen if the requirements of computer software will have an influence too.

Looking at the neologisms used to talk about video gaming in Irish above, I considered the various ways a new word can be formed. Sometimes a term for technology can come from a piece of literature. For example, the word 'robot' entered English from *robotnik*, a Czech word for a slave that was popularized in a play called *Rossum's Universal Robots* by Karel Čapek.

Tearma.ie has over one hundred Irish-language entries in its robotics category. A compliant robot, for example, is a **róbat comhlíontach**. The Irish for self-motion is **féinghluaisne** (you might recognize **féin** and **gluaisteán** in that one). Some of them are almost musical; hazardous motion, for example, is the alluringly alliterative **gluaisne ghuaiseach**.

Ecophagy (consumption/destruction of life by sentient technology) is **gú glas** in Irish – literally, grey goo. Combat robotics is **comhrac róbataice**.

A fembot (yes, really) is **bota baineann**. The idea of robots imitating humans too closely repulses some. There are three listed Irish translations for uncanny valley, the repulsion humans feel toward almost-human systems.

Áit ait – weird place

Gleann gránna – ugly hollow / glen

Dúiche déistine – nausea area

Is there an uncanny valley at play regarding the similarity of the English scientific terms to the Irish ones? Well, some of them are quite similar – swarm robotics is **róbataic saithe** – and some of them are not – replicator is **macasamhlóir**, which sounds like a surname, and sensory feedback is **aisfhotha céadfach**.

Robonaut is **spásróbat** – space robot. A programmable robot (you'd like to think they're all programmable at this stage) is a **róbat inríomhchláraithe**. Therefore, a programmable robonaut is a **spásróbat inríomhchláraithe**.

Wearable robot is **róbat inchaite** – not to be confused with **róba inchaite**, wearable robe. Another linguistic banana skin to watch out for: **cibé** (whoever / whichever) is not the same as **cibearg** (cyborg). The spelling of **cibearg** may be close to the English word, but it's pronounced with a hard C in Irish.

When I was a child, every office desk had an ashtray and computers had tape decks. When I joined the workforce, you couldn't make a phone call and use the Internet at the same time. Now I'm raising my daughter in a world where humans are being expected to act more and more like machines, working jobs with increasingly precise processes, scripted customer services answers, shorter breaks and the expectation to be on call at all times. It is also a world where machines are expected to be more and more human, making decisions and interpreting customer personality traits. I can only imagine how much will have

changed by the time she finishes school. When that time
comes around, will the machines have finally taken all the
jobs – even those of the translators?

——×Ⅲ×Ⅲ×—— Machine translation ——×Ⅲ×Ⅲ×——

Some months back a Twitter user sent me a screen grab
of Google Translate – someone they followed had made
a comment in Irish followed by the words 'an RA abú!'.
Google Translate rendered these words as 'Hooray for the
UK!'.

Many readers will know that RA is, in Hiberno-English,
an abbreviation of IRA; unfortunately, the Irish for the
United Kingdom is **an Ríocht Aontaithe**... RA for short.

First of all, it needs to be said that RA as an abbreviation of IRA isn't actually an Irish word. This is a good
example of the problems associated with a lack of a formal
dictionary of Hiberno-English. For a machine to be able
to translate from one language to another is tricky enough
without having to make a judgement call on the loanwords
presented to it. Having a corpus of English words particular to Ireland would be useful supplementary information.
Having said that, loanwords are hardly the only stumbling
block preventing Google Translate and similar technology
from working seamlessly.

From their humble origins in the Cold War when linguists laboriously encoded grammatical rules into gigantic
computers, machine-based translators are getting more
and more sophisticated. In particular the capacity to

understand the meaning of a word in context is increasing – routine phrases such as 'baby changing room' can be correctly identified and not confused with a room where one baby is traded for another. They can do this because of the increased use of data-driven techniques (referencing a body of previously translated work) to supplement rule-based techniques (identifying past and present tenses of the same verb, word order, the significance of capitalization and so on).

Data-driven techniques feed a machine translator with as much bilingual data as possible from previously translated documents – novels, articles, government reports, online conversations and so on. From this body of data, patterns can be identified and learned. The translation machine understands that the sentence fragment 'Welcome to Connolly Station' is welcoming the visitor, not the station. It comes to realize that Air France is referring to a business rather than the air in France. And it is better at figuring out what a sentence means if a word is missing or misspelled.

In order to do this well, a machine translator needs thousands and thousands of translated documents. This quantity of resources is not available in Irish to designers of machine translation software, and its absence is sorely felt. This is one of the reasons Microsoft has not yet offered Irish as one of the languages in Bing, its translation package. This is the one used by Twitter.

The non-inclusion of Irish in Bing's service means that when people tweet in Irish, Twitter is unable to work out what language is being used and has to guess from the resources available to it. For example, the Irish word for 'other', **eile**, is spelled the same way as the Estonian word for 'yesterday'. The Irish word for 'things', **rudaí**, means 'rope' in Slovak.

But there are not always entire word matches. These systems use n-grams, which are combinations of letters within words – unigrams (one letter), bigrams (two letters), trigrams (three letters) and so on. Certain trigram combinations are particular to two languages or even to one. Based on a 26-letter alphabet, there are over 17,500 possible trigrams, which is more than the number of languages in use today. So an *mbl* or a *bdb* could narrow an entire piece of text down to Irish very quickly... if Irish were included.

However, even if Bing added Irish tomorrow, it wouldn't be the end of the workload. Just as we learn to drive on quiet roads or empty car parks, machine translation technology learns its work from 'proper' texts, which are different from the way people speak to each other. The language used in Tumblr posts, Facebook status updates and tweets is full of spelling errors, abbreviations and cavalier punctuation. Learning from this content is just as valuable, as instinctive trends in abbreviation just might tell us something valuable about who we are and how we think.

In Tom Stoppard's play *Arcadia*, a girl in 1809 comes close to hitting on a mathematical breakthrough that isn't discovered for another 160 years. Discovering her journals, a character remarks that in mathematics, the invention of 'the electronic calculator was what the telescope was for Galileo... she'd only have to press a button, the same button over and over. Iteration. A few minutes. And what I've done in a couple of months, with only a pencil the calculations would take me the rest of my life to do again'.

Machine translation isn't coming to replace the work of humans, but it is creating great opportunities for them to work faster, speeding through the repetitive parts of long technical documents and allowing trained professionals to spend more time on the creative, decision-making side of the process. It can also lead to rapid translation in times of crisis.

The best way for Irish speakers and enthusiasts to help machine translators to get better right now is to update Wikipedia's Irish-language site, Vicipéid. At the time of writing the Irish language portion is smaller than that of Breton, a far less used language. If every Honours Irish student in the Leaving Cert cycle (Fifth and Sixth Years) wrote two articles on whatever subject they wished (favourite sports team, book, album, whatever), the amount of content available could be almost doubled.

A more richly populated Vicipéid might also help prevent the confusion that similar-sounding words with different meanings can invite. Consider the following:

Anghrá means erotic... not to be confused with angora, a niche variety of wool.

Callóid means noise and commotion... as opposed to **cuallóid**, which means a boisterous gal.

Westmeath is **an Iarmhí**... but an **iarmhó** is a great-grandchild.

Imeartas means playfulness... as opposed to **iomartas**, which means supernatural influence.

Dream means a group of people – a tribe, a demographic or a crowd. It doesn't mean dream... except possibly a dream team.

One of the words in Irish for electricity is **aibhléis**... quite unlike **aibhéis**, the dark abyss.

Lúireach (a prayer for protection) couldn't possibly get mixed up with **liúireach** (shouting or yelling), could it?

―×⫼×⫼×― **Double meanings...** ―×⫼×⫼×―

The Irish word for innuendo is **claontagairt**. Sorry it's so long and hard.

The prefix **tuath-** can mean rural, on the left side... or evil. As a noun in its own right, **tuath** means tribe or people and may also refer (historically) to a little kingdom.

Cloigeann can mean (among other things) a skull, a roof or the head of a pint.

Lost property is **earra caillte**. Interestingly, **caillte** can also mean sordid or very bad.

Soiprigh is the verb to snuggle. It can also refer to the practice of getting wrapped up or nesting.

—×Ⅲ×Ⅲ×— **Not to be confused...** —×Ⅲ×Ⅲ×—

An earring is a **fáinne cluaise**. Not to be confused with an **arraing**, a stabbing pain.

An **ainle** (a brat or squirrel) is not to be confused with an **áinle**, a swallow (which is where the female given name comes from).

Taerthó means remark, and is not to be confused with Tayto, the popular brand of crisp.

An **alltán** (monster or wild man) should not be confused with a **scalltán** (a tiny, puny creature like a nestling).

One of the several Irish words for smooth is **socair**... not to be confused with soccer, a popular and lucrative sport.

Táthán means cement and is not to be confused with **an t-áthán**, which refers to one's arse.

The Irish for Prohibition (the period in US history when the 18th Amendment and Volstead Act were in force) is **an Cosc ar Alcól**. Speaking of alcohol, the Irish for food is **bia**, not to be confused with the Australian pronunciation of beer.

—×Ⅲ×Ⅲ×Ⅲ×— **Literally...** —×Ⅲ×Ⅲ×Ⅲ×—

One of the Irish words for bookmark is **ga leabhair**, which translates literally as book spear. The other is **leabharmharc** (**leabhar** book, **marc** mark), which is just a bit too **ar an tsrón** for me.

A **drochbhraon** – literally, bad drop – is a negative inherited trait.

One of the Irish terms for small change is **airgead briste**, literally broken money.

Tartfheoil means tough, dried-up meat (literally thirsty meat).

Sméar is blackberry. It's easy to remember because they leave a smear on your hands and lips when you eat them.

The Irish for suave is **síodúil**. A suave fellow would be a **síodóg**. However, a **slaisire** is a slasher (one who slashes, in combat or agriculture). It may also mean a presentable, charming man or animal.

One of the words for duality is **déacht**... not to be confused with **éacht**, which refers to a fine achievement or an utter slaying.

Ainscian means large knife. It can also mean fury, extravagance or furious/wild person.

Uallfartach means howling or yelling; it has nothing to do with apples or farting.

The Irish for my candle is **mo choinneal**... not to be confused with **modh coinníollach**.

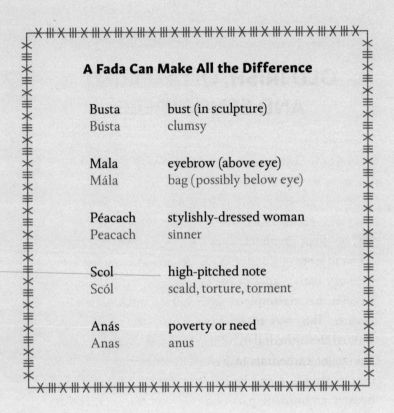

A Fada Can Make All the Difference

Busta	bust (in sculpture)
Bústa	clumsy
Mala	eyebrow (above eye)
Mála	bag (possibly below eye)
Péacach	stylishly-dressed woman
Peacach	sinner
Scol	high-pitched note
Scól	scald, torture, torment
Anás	poverty or need
Anas	anus

OLD IRISH, OLDER IRISH AND SENGOÍDELC

~⌒

The great architect Gaudí was a passionate Catalan and lover of Catalan traditions who famously died in the very early stages of the construction of the Sagrada Família, his masterpiece that dominates the Barcelona skyline. This was to be expected, however, as Gaudí wanted the cathedral to be built on a medieval timeframe. The major cathedrals in European cities had been built over generations, and he felt that this meant a cathedral became an intimate part of a city's history – a grandson finishing a grandfather's work, the job slowing down and speeding up depending on the fortunes of the land, the materials available and the skills learned.

The fact that an unfinished cathedral could be the largest thing in a city for a century would gently remind citizens that good things take time. And with the current stirrings in Europe, Gaudí's masterpiece might be finally finished in an independent Catalonia.

Much like the Sagrada Família, the Irish language is a work in progress and different parts come from different points in history, when Irish society had different cultural tastes, economic priorities and attitudes to life. There's often a bit of faux traditionalism about Irish (even from people who don't speak it), and some readers may find some of the words for modern technology I've shared so far to be a bit inauthentic. I've heard time and time again the view that certain letters or words shouldn't be used in Irish and that it should be kept the way it's always been.

However, it hasn't been any one way for too long. It might be useful to take a long look back to see how far we've come.

Who wants some Old Irish words? I don't just mean the stuff from a hundred years ago (even though that's objectively old), but Sengoídelc, the Irish from the middle ages. I have some examples for you, and some proverbs too. Some of them give an insight into a different world. I'll also look at the technological innovations used in researching these texts.

Sengoídelc is substantially different from modern Irish in its grammar and pronunciation conventions, so I don't propose that Irish learners use these words in their homework or in conversation. The objective is to give a taste of what has changed and what hasn't.

Ócán is an Old Irish word for a young lad, preserved in the medieval rhyme *Cride Hé*:

Cride hé	He's a heart
Daire cnó	A grove of nuts/nut trees
Ócán é	He's a young lad
Pócán do.	A kiss for him.

Clearly this is more of a 'he loves me, he loves me not' rhyme than some profound literary feat, and I'm glad it has survived. It's always nice to remember that in the ninth century, first crushes and the equivalent of playground rhymes were already a thing. **Ócán** is no longer in use; dropping it into your conversational Irish would be like dropping **beadufolm** (hand-to-hand combat) or **beclypping** (an embrace) into your conversational English. The descendant of **ócán** in modern Irish is **ógánach**. One of the charming parts of this verse is rhyming the word for young lad with the word for kiss – **pócán** survives in modern Irish as a word you'll certainly recognize, **póg**.

Némann means pearl or a precious stone, not to be confused with Nemain, an Irish war goddess married to Néit, a war god. What did they talk about at home? Who knows.

The turn of phrase for describing someone with nice

teeth – **ba fras de némannaib boí ina bélaib** – literally translates as 'a shower of pearls that was in her mouth'. A phrase
with the same sentiment exists in modern Irish too, but it's
spelled **a déad mar fhras néamhann,** which hints at how
much the language has changed. The word hasn't changed
that much from Old Irish to modern Irish, so you'd be forgiven for thinking other words for pearl in Irish are cheesy
blow-ins. However, **pérla** was used by no less a luminary
than Seathrún Céitinn (Geoffrey Keating)* in the seven-
teenth century, reminding us that loanwords are nothing
new.

* Seathrún Céitinn, anglicised as Geoffrey Keating, is one of
the major writers in pre-revival Irish. After studying abroad
to become a priest, he returned to Ireland after the Flight of
the Earls, the event credited with precipitating the decline
of Gaelic Ireland. His major work is *Foras Feasa ar Éirinn*
(History of Ireland).

Drúcht

Drúcht means dew and has survived in modern Irish with
the same spelling. I mention it partly to show that some
words have held their shape, but also to consider some
turns of phrase it pops up in. **Drúchta Dea**, the dew of a
goddess, is a kenning for corn. There's an intriguing line of
poetry: *A chumainn is a searc, rachaimid-ne seal faoi choillte ag
scaipeadh drúchta* (My love and desire, let us go and scatter
the dew in the woods).

Armchar means weapon-loving, not to be confused with armchair, a piece of furniture. This one is from *The Metrical Dindshenchas** but it's unclear if the word was widely used in speech at the time or coined by an eloquent scribe. Modern readers with any Irish at all will recognize **chara** as meaning friend – this word (**arm + chara**) is derived from that and is a kind of kenning.

If you've read *Beowulf*, you might already be familiar with kennings, elegant two-word figures of speech that stand in for words which might otherwise be repeated too frequently for the purposes of an epic poem. Referring to a river as the swan road or the sky as the lark land would be examples of this. These poetic word pairings are especially popular in old Irish. Here's a dramatic one for a weapon: **áilleagán na n-airdríogh** (darling/plaything of high kings). Continuing on that theme, **rígdomna** means heir-apparent – literally, material of a king.

Nemed mbled means the sea and translates literally as the sanctuary of whales, a kenning with a nice rhyme and a suitably watery onomatopoeia. These words have descendants in modern Irish; the word for sanctuary

* Dindsenchas means the lore of places and is a major historical text for students of Old and Middle Irish. Historical events are sometimes listed without obvious reference to each other or with striking switches in significance, going from describing a battle to giving an account of a cow who gave birth to four calves. In this regard it has similarities to a social media newsfeed.

is **neimheadh,** and **bleidhmhíol** is one of the words for a whale. **Bleidhmhíol** (**bleidh** + **míol**) is a curiosity, as **míol** on its own can also mean whale. Whale oil is **míolúsc**... not to be confused with mollusc.

Ruidles is that quintessential quality specific to someone, the peculiar property, right or characteristic of a person or thing. In modern Irish, it would be **ródhílis.**

Asoilgi laith lochrúna – Ale reveals dark secrets. Not just ale, of course, wine too. A nice fancy term for wine in Irish is **sú na fíniúna** (juice of the grapevine).

In Old Irish, **cais** could mean both love and hate (in modern Irish it's just hate).

Dubén

Félithir dubén means as generous as a black bird (possibly a crow or raven, rather than specifically a blackbird). The implication is that birds such as crows and ravens summon their peers upon finding food, unlike other birds who stop singing when they feed. It's possible that this noble trait was poorly estimated by the Old Irish; *Dinneen* defines **faingín** as 'tall, good-for-nothing girl' and this is derived from **faing**, raven.

You might recognize **dubén** as looking a bit like the modern words **dubh** (black) and **éan** (bird). Of course, in modern Irish the adjective would come after the noun – the style here is much like the root of Dublin (**dubh** and **linn** – black pool).

Ritire, the word for knight or horseman, hasn't changed too much – the modern spelling is **ridire**. One of the more noteworthy **ridire** from Irish mythology is **An Ridire Dubhach Gan Gháire** – The Knight Without a Laugh. When asked why he didn't laugh, he explained that he and his sons were out hunting and chased a hare into a cave. Once inside the cave, they were set upon by ogres (the hare had been a shapeshifter sent to trick them) who submitted them to repeated humiliations such as pulling ropes, washing pigs and over-eating to the point where the sons choked on bones.

Blinne is a girl's name which translates literally as dead person's spittle. For some reason it is no longer widely used.

Oíbell is an old word for a seed of fire – an ember or a spark. It could also refer to a person: the old **seanfhocal** (proverb) **ná séit oíbell cen atúd** means don't waste your breath blowing on an ember with no flame left in it. An **oíbelteóir** is a hermit or recluse.

Ní raib clann ná cenélach, rub dérechtach díbdathach! is an alliterative Sengoídelc curse requesting that some-one be left abandoned and childless. A lot of importance was placed on curses in Gaelic Ireland, with huge stock placed in reputation and insults taken very seriously. This is reflected in the concept of **corrguinecht**, which trans-lates literally as heron killing – killing (figuratively) in the style of a heron, not killing herons! This was a pose adopted by druids when performing a curse or satire, standing on one leg with one eye closed and one arm out. But the real druid bird wasn't the heron, it was the wren.

 **Sagart**

Another constant feature in Irish, one that hasn't changed for centuries while the language around it has moved onward, is the word **sagart** (a priest), still spelled as it was before the Reformation. Have attitudes to them stayed constant too? Consider this couplet:

*Ní chreidim go bráth ó shagart nó ó bhráthair
Go bhfuil peaca ins an pháirt a dhúbladh.*

These are the last lines of a seventeenth-century poem sometimes called 'My Fairest Girl' (the elusiveness of true poem titles from this period is the bane of scholars' lives, and often opening lines are used). Thomas Kinsella has translated them as:

No priest or friar will I believe
That it's sin to couple in love.

Lechtach, as well as meaning liquid, can refer to a place strewn with memorial cairns and grave mounds. It persists in modern Irish as **leachtach**.

 **Somewhat old**

These words aren't Old Irish, they're just Irish and old. They've fallen out of regular use, friends only to the dictionaries of yesterday. Some of them could be useful today; for example, while the Irish for Aunt is **aintín,** older dictionaries helpfully list different terms for maternal and paternal aunts (**máithreán** and **athaireog**). Others are more like windows into a different time.

Ilrinceadh – a ball, promiscuous dance. Nobody puts *O'Reilly's Dictionary* in a corner.

Lurgfhurc is a word with two syllables, but what does it mean? It means a word with two syllables. If you think that joke is cheesy, you're not alone: none of the other dictionaries I use thought **lurgfhurc** was good enough to include. Poor **lurgfhurc**.

Mac salach – literally, dirty lad – is an old name for a toad which is sadly missed.

Luchlann – mouse / vermin place – is an obscure but stunning word for a prison from *O'Reilly*. It follows the format of **bialann** (restaurant (food place)) and **leabharlann** (library (book place)). I can't find earlier or later citations of **luchlann**, so maybe don't use it in your homework unless it's a piece of creative writing. **Carcair / príosún** are more widely used terms for prison.

A mouse-hole is an **ábhach luiche**; pun-lovers will note that **ábhach** (hole or recess) is irresistibly similar to **ábhacht** (jest or banter). A **páideog** (little paddy) can mean a young mouse or a person who eats untidily. Finally, speaking of abodes and vermin, **fialteagh** (a place where ferrets are bred) isn't in the *foclóir* anymore. Not to be confused with **fáilteach**, which means welcoming.

Bascaire doesn't have an exact match in English; it's a

round of clapping performed mournfully.

Crúite means milked, literally or figuratively; Father Dinneen describes it as being 'deprived of one's secret [or] money... by a gradual process'.

A hostage is a **giall**. This isn't especially obscure; it's the name of the original Irish version of Brendan Behan's *The Hostage*. However, a counter-hostage is a **frith-ghiall**. The prefix **frith**- means anti- or counter-, and is not to be confused with **frith**, a stray or finding (**goid fríotha** means theft by finding).

In his seminal dictionary, Father Dinneen defines **caistín** as:

'a crafty little fellow;

a little girl of prematurely old appearance or manner;

a vicious person;

a potato shrivelled from frost or heat;

a speckled little bird believed to spend the greater part of the year in a state of torpidity'.

Here are some other entries from *Dinneen* which show his unique flourish:

As well as meaning sleeping and mating, **feis** also once referred to trespassing (of livestock) in a cornfield.

Uiscefhuaraithe describes someone or something that has been cooled in water.

A **dóigh** is an object or thing to be hunted / frequented / meddled with / made free with; a place where one expects to find what one seeks. **Cuarduigh dóigh is an-dóigh dhe**: search it all, likely and unlikely places. **Ní haon dóigh é**: he's no joke, he's not to be trifled with.

Fraighleachar means ooze from walls.

Strae is also often used to refer to a stray animal; it and 'stray' appear to have entered Irish and English from Norman French. Stray boulders are a different story, though. **Duirling** doesn't have an exact match in English; it means a row of boulders thrown up on the coast by storm or tide.

A **finndhabaigh** is a counterfeit sigh.

A **fuairtnín** is a sterile she-goat.

An explosion is a **pléasc**.

FANTASY ISLAND

The Irish for immigration is **inimirce**, which sounds poetically close to 'America' after an ale or two. Ireland's relationship with America and Irish-Americans has been instrumental in creating its idea of itself. This relationship is now in flux as the political priorities of Irish America pivot away from what we previously understood them to be.

In Ireland, there has long been a warped smugness in regard to the affection Irish-Americans have for this island, or what they imagine it to be. This isn't always picked up by tourists but is never missed by Irish-Americans who have lived here for a year or more. Stories about gullible Americans and their misguided remarks – crimes like an inability to tell the difference between a County Laois accent and a Portlaoise accent,* or maybe being unfamiliar with the

---

* I could write a whole other book on Irish accents and the depth of feeling provoked in their defence. The attempts >>

two-part pour – are practically icebreakers when groups of Irish people meet. This is followed by remarks confirming that Ireland isn't really the way they think it is, but that the misconception doesn't do us or them any harm.

The postcard image of Ireland – Irish dancing at crossroads, pints and fiddles, pastoral poverty – patronizes us, but it flatters us too. The idea that American interest in Ireland may have peaked and that they know fine well that it's not like *The Quiet Man* anymore won't butter any sandwiches.

I say this at the outset because in order to talk properly about Irish and authenticity, it's critical that we don't fall into the trap of nodding smugly at the misunderstandings of others. I don't want to get into an 'Americans think this about Ireland but we know better' tailspin, because that doesn't get to the truth of things. It's only natural for a person's interest in another country to focus on the exciting and colourful parts of its history, and there's no reason why an American tourist in green trousers should be expected to have a detailed knowledge of Ireland that exceeds the detailed knowledge of the Czech Republic held by Irish

>> by Hollywood movie stars to mimic Irish accents is a well of cheap laughs that I won't live to see run dry – the dramatic achievements of Tom Cruise, Richard Gere and Julia Roberts in their other roles will never eclipse their attempts to play Irish people in films that none of them probably even remember making. What's jarring is that there's so little praise for the international stars who put the effort in to get an Irish accent right.

stag parties in Prague. Of course, if those American tourists choose to find out more about Ireland and Irish, they will open a treasure chest of the mind; I envy them getting to read certain stories and word meanings for the first time, and we should all wish them well on their way.

For all the slagging that Irish-Americans get in Ireland, the view throughout my lifetime has been that they're a fundamentally decent bunch and their contribution to American life has been substantial and honourable. Like so many people in Ireland, I was alarmed to see the long list of Irish names in President Trump's team – Ryan, Bannon, Conway and the rest. We were used to thinking of Irish-American politicians as liberal pragmatists from the northeast, people generally on the right side of history – the Kennedy clan, Senator George Morrison, Tip O'Neill and so on.

The new batch are different.

Authenticity is a lot like modesty; it's a concept that resists its own conscious existence. The effort required to be modest or authentic, or to realize that you're doing it well, demonstrates that a performance is required, that these qualities are not inherent. Flann O'Brien observed that all modesty must be false modesty, because a truly modest person would not consider their actions modest or seek the approval that modesty invites.

So it goes with authenticity: we live our lives in traffic jams, in meetings or plonked in front of computer screens, craving something more real while reality is all too present.

Authenticity can hold opposite meanings – we can know and reject the authenticity of our own lives and seek a type of reality that fits more closely to our idea of what reality should actually be.

The Irish language and associated points of Irish culture here (such as Gaelic sports, Irish dancing and music) straddle the authenticity problem in personal and political ways. One of the factors motivating the various movements to increase the use and acceptance of Gaeilge has been the sense that it's one of the things that make us unique. Without Irish, Ireland might be indistinguishable from a lump of Massachusetts (or perhaps even Lancashire) that came loose and drifted across the Atlantic. This uniqueness hasn't always been appreciated by schoolchildren, whose search for authenticity led elsewhere – to career options, to immediate gratification, to a more kindly-marked school subject, to a different personal passion.

Across the Atlantic and in pockets around the world, people who never had to study the Irish language under the looming shadow of a nun or a Christian Brother have taken an interest in it. Free of such school memories, all they see is the beauty – and, yes, the authenticity – of the words, the phrases and the music.

But how authentic is this search for authenticity?

The story of prosperous, jaded individuals from wealthy societies taking an interest in the culture of poorer, 'purer' ones is neither new nor unique to Irish. This interest can often be purely decorative and a little patronizing; but

it can also be sincere and deeply felt. In fact, it can be instrumental to the survival and greater understanding of a culture.

Learning Irish in these circumstances can lead to a Grecian urn problem. You're fascinated by something mysterious, strange and beautiful; but studying it makes it less mysterious and less strange. Does it make it less beautiful?

ϒϒϒ Decorative Irish – Tattoos ϒϒϒ

It's not unfair to say that some people's interest in the Irish language doesn't extend to a commitment to obtaining perfect conversational fluency. However, some of them are prepared to make a lifelong commitment to the language by having it added to their own skin. In this regard, the pre-modern Irish font joins the ranks of Japanese, Hebrew and Mandarin in looking cool enough to spend a lifetime on an arm or back.

Before we rush to ridicule this trend, let's consider its appeal. First of all, there are reasonable circumstances in which a person might get a tattoo in a language they don't speak – US marines might choose to get a SEMPER FI tattoo, even if they don't speak Latin. People with a connection to another military body or organization (a school or city, perhaps) might be similarly moved to commit to a Latin motto.

Secondly, consider this. If an English speaker tattooed the words 'I Am a Beautiful Princess' on their lower back, or 'Very Strong and Brave Warrior who Protects Women' on their bicep, this would be far too on-the-nose for most. A Chinese symbol meaning either of these things might be more aesthetically pleasing than the English letters. Also, if it involves fewer characters, it will be easier to tattoo and fit to the chosen body part.

Thirdly, the fact that the meaning isn't immediately obvious to most may be deliberate. Maybe the bearer getting to decide with whom they share the meaning is part of the appeal. The exception here is people who speak the language in question, in which case the tattoo-bearer might be pleased to make their acquaintance.

Now that we've set the ground rules for what is deemed acceptable, let's torch everything else to the ground. Firstly, there are speed limits on all the grounds for exceptions above. If you want words inked onto your skin in a language you don't speak, how strongly do you really feel about those words? Would you wear henna of the words in English for a whole week? If you expect most people who see your tattoo not to understand it, what does that say about that language's role in your life? If you think the words are too cheesy in English, I'm confident that an Irish speaker will find them too cheesy in Irish too.

What I'm saying is, don't get 'May the force be with you' tattooed on your arm in Irish. If you feel an urge to get an Irish tattoo and no urge to learn Irish, consider a pre-existing line from a song or a work of literature.

For example:

1. **Subh Milis** is one of the best-loved Irish language poems, and the symbolism of the handprint in it, or an extract

from it, makes it ideally suited to a tattoo. Here's the full poem by Séamus Ó'Néill:

Bhí subh milis	there's sweet jam
Ar bhaschrann an dorais	on the door handle
Ach mhúch mé an corraí	but I quench the rage
Ionam d'éirigh,	rising in me
Mar smaoinigh mé ar an lá	because I think of the day
A bheas an bhaschrann glan,	that the handle will be clean
Agus an láimh bheag	and the little hand
Ar iarraidh.	missing/gone.

2. **Táimid caillte sa cheo chéanna** – we're lost in the same mist. This one is from Nuala Ní Dhomhnaill's poem Ualach an Uaignis and is an elegant way of describing kindred spirits.

3. **Dar Liom, Is Galar É An Ghrádh** – Love, I think is a disease – might be more suitable to those more cynical (though no less susceptible) towards matters of the heart. From the poem of the same name by Maghnas Ó Domhnaill.

4. **An sgéal fada ní hé is fearr** – the longest tale is not the best. Advice for life there, and surely the perfect tattoo for any editor. From the anonymous love poem *Gluais, A Litir, Ná Leig Sgís.*

5. **C.E.A.R.T.A. Is Cuma Liom Sa Foc Faoi Aon Gharda** – *(Rights – I don't give a fuck about any police officer)* The most modern entry is a line from the chorus of the song C.E.A.R.T.A. by Belfast hip-hop act Kneecap, who

have applied gangsta rap tropes to their Irish language compositions.

If those are too fancy for you, there's some in the next section which are a bit more metal.

⟁⟁⟁⟁⟁⟁⟁ Celtic Fantasy ⟁⟁⟁⟁⟁⟁

The land **Fóthuinn** is described in *Dinneen's Dictionary* as 'a country in romance'. No more details are given, and the reader can only speculate as to what kind of romances were set in this mysterious land.

My wife's hometown of Ballycastle and the surrounding area have enjoyed a surge in tourism lately, on account of *Game of Thrones* fans wanting to visit its outdoor filming locations. Fantasy literature has been consistently popular since I was a child, but that particular show and book series have led to a sharp spike in interest. *Game of Thrones* has even been translated into Irish under the title ***Cluiche na Corónach***.

The search for suitable settings has led some authors to consider using pre-existing Irish mythology tropes as a story palette – and with words like these, sure who could blame them?

* *Fíon geal* (white wine) is not to be confused with Fine Gael (a political party).

Fionaíolach is kin-slayer, not to be confused with **fíontach*** (abounding in, or fond of, wine) or **fionnaitheach**, an old word for furry.

Eirleach means carnage... not to be confused with **meirleach**, outlaw or villain. **Bithiúnach** can also mean villain.

Craorag is one of the Irish words for crimson or blood-red. This can also refer to drinking whiskey neat (**fuisce a ól craorag**).

The obscure noun and adjective **tonn-fhola** refers to bloody waves.

Fuildoirteadh means bloodshed – it's a compound of **fuil** (blood) and **doirteadh** (pouring / spilling).

Cíocras is one of the Irish words for greed; **ciocrus fola flannrúaidhe** (pre-modern spelling) means hunger for red, red blood.

Partardeirg is a word for crimson from old Irish heroic literature, derived from **partaing** (Parthian, referring to a region in modern-day Iran).

Diúc means duke and is certainly not to be confused with **diúcach**, a sly boyo.

Éachtach means killer... not to be confused with **eachtrach**, adventurous or eventful.

An **airbe druad**, literally a druidic hedge, is a kind of magic force field.

ⵋⵋⵋⵋⵋⵋⵋ Druids! Druids! ⵋⵋⵋⵋⵋⵋⵋ

Ard-draoi means archdruid... not to be confused with the similarly pronounced **ard-rí**, high king. You couldn't really have a fantasy novel set in Ireland without a druid or two; they're basically pagan wizards, right?

Perhaps. At one point it was a general term for any pagan clerics anywhere – Bishop O'Brien describes Egyptian high priests as druids in his dictionary. In light of this, and the levels of literacy at the time, it's unlikely that druidism was a single belief system with defined and defended positions. And while there certainly were ritual specialists of many kinds in Old Ireland, archaeological evidence for druids remains to be seen. However, there are still people going around today who self-identify as druids and practise paganism with a Celtic* twist.

Some months back a text called *An Foclóir Draíochta* (Druid Dictionary, or Magic Dictionary) was brought to my attention. It proposes to assist ADF (short for A Druid Fellowship but also **Ár nDraíocht Féin**) druids perform rituals by offering relevant Irish terminology. I haven't verified the origin or authenticity of this text,† but its definitions give an impression of what being a druid is all about:

- The entry for Pádraig (the patron saint of Ireland credited with Christianizing the island) sassily dismisses him as a 'Welsh evangelist'. All Old Irish words beginning with P are borrowed (Latin or British Celtic). In the fifth century, P was so foreign that it took the Irish several generations to learn its pronunciation. Take that, Saint Patrick!

---

* The influence of the Celts in Ireland may have been dramatically overstated in the 17th and 18th centuries.

† Seriously, lads – I'm presenting this as a curiosity only.

- **Draoi Ríogaí** (court druids) are contrasted with **Draoi Allta** (non-court druids). The lexicographer clearly sides with the latter: 'The adjective refers to wildness and not crazy / violent and connotates [sic] amazement.' Although it isn't pointed out in this particular text, **altar / an t-alltar** can mean the otherworld as well as a remote place. Our lexicographer adds that **draoi ríogaí** are toadies and their name is a pun on 'royalist and most spasmodic'.

- **Dílmain Drong**, 'the restraint of crowds', is defined as conformity to a common social mindset. The lexicographer adds that **bándraíocht** (white magic) is the practice of 'fake druidism drained dry of genuine elements, or diluted of difficulty to be popular'.

- **Athdholb** is one's shape-shifted form. If shapeshifting is your game, it's easy to forget which self is real. It's unclear what Irish words this term shape shifted from.

- A **lionn iomhais** is 'a drink granting magical insight'.

- A **suantraí** is a harp strain to (magically) induce sleep. This is in the real dictionary as the word for a lullaby.

- **Beannú na déithe's n'aindhéithe ort** is a druid pleasantry that translates as 'The blessings of the gods and the non-gods upon you'. This expression is noted in the *Táin*.

· A **glám díceann** is a short, exhibitionistic, magical satire. This one must be the work of a **draoi allot**, as they refuse to obey courtly grammar rules: **glám** – grab / clutch / tear; **dícheann** – behead.

The job status and work conditions of druids (including sick leave) were badly affected by the advance of Christianity. One law text, the *Bretha Crólige* from the eighth century, states that druids were now only entitled to the level of sick maintenance appropriate to a satirist or brigand. There was a long overlap between the fall of druidism and the rise of Christianity, and during this time druids went from being highly respected to highly feared.

A lot of what we know about druids, or even the spectrum of pagan practices that we carelessly group together under the umbrella of that term, is filtered through misperceptions, but also through fictional works set in the period. Such works always say more about the era in which they were written than they do about their subject.

Consider two examples – oak and mistletoe. While druids had nothing against the **crann darach** (oak), it was not sacred to them; the rowan, **caorthann**, was. The people who were really mad into oak trees were the British navy, whose ship builders needed waterproof timber. The idea that British sea power was built from oak trees that were disappearing across the countryside gave some artists and writers cause to see the tree sentimentally, and they were attracted to the idea that it has stored British power under its bark all along, right back to Arthurian times. Similarly, botanists reckon that there was no more mistletoe in pagan Ireland than there were snakes.

The fun-to-say **anuasal** means a person of low birth. Given that **na huaisle** can mean fairy folk, it could mean a mere mortal.

While a **coileán** is a puppy, *Dinneen* tells us that a **coileán uasal** is an enchanted whelp. Speaking of dogs, the recherché word **coinreacht** is tucked away in *Dinneen's foclóir* and sadly overlooked by later texts – it means laws relating to dogs. Another doggo word, **fearchú**, means a male dog / hound, or a man as impressive as a dog.

The most famous dog-like man in Irish mythology is Cuchulainn, who was capable of entering warp spasms when enraged: this state was called a **ríastrad**, which could also refer to a similarly dramatic transformation or distortion.

An **aosán** is an evil fairy or spirit in Irish. They're absolute feckers.

Falscaí (mountain fire) is not to be confused with **falchaí** (mean, spiteful). There's no direct equivalent in English to **aduantas an tsléibhe**, which *Dinneen* translates as the loneliness of the mountain.

A **teach siúil** – walking / moving house – is a haunted house. One of the Irish words for spooky is **scáfar**; another is **taibhsiúil** (ghostly).

Ruchsaidhe are the sayings or words of the dead... uttered while they were alive, presumably.

A blood cell is **cill fola**. Interestingly, **cill** can also mean church. Blood rain (rain that contains enough red sand to colour it) is **ruabháisteach**.

The adjective **goibéalta** means pointed, sharp or sarcastic. It can also describe very fresh air.

There's a few words for crow in Irish. One is **badhbh** (rhymes with Sadhbh), which is also the name of a Celtic war goddess.

Fáthrúnda means mystical or mysterious.

A **maochrán** is a beautiful woman, so beautiful that she just might be from the faerie world. A better-known term is **spéirbhean** – sky woman.

Brichtscribhenna briste catha are spell writings that win battles.

The adjective **doilfe** means occult, mystical or magical.

Eachtraí are adventures or fabulous occurrences.

Another translation given for bogeyman is **taibhse an chnádáin**. **Cnádán** can mean bur, leech, thistle or toad, and a **taibhse** is a ghost.

One of the Irish words for witchcraft (of course there's a few) is **asarlaíocht**. However, a witch in the non-fairytale context is **bean feasa** – wise woman.

Geal means bright or white; **gealach** means moon, and a **seanghealach** is a waning moon. The word for solstice is **grianstad** (**grian**: sun, **stad**: stop).

A dark secret is a **dúrún**. A dark horse is a **capall anaithnid** – an unnamed horse.

One of the Irish words for destiny is **cinniúint**.

To **ainligh** means to hold steady against strong winds or currents.

A **dallsíon** is a blinding storm – the perfect time for ghost stories.

One of the Irish words for fairytale is **síscéal**. As well as being the name of a once-famous Munster fairy, a **clíodhna** can mean a person wasting away from sickness. **Friothóir na Rátha** is an old Connacht term for the head fairy of a fairy fort (a **ráth** is a regular fort, and the prefix **frioth-** means anti- or counter-). **Liosachán** is another word for a fairy fort. Even people who aren't especially superstitious are reluctant to mess around with these.

A **púca** is a cheeky, mischievous imp. This one is easy to remember for fans of a Midsummer Night's Dream and Dublin's most prettily named water reservoir, Poula-phouca (Poll an Phúca, the Imp's Cave).

The Irish for imaginary is **samhailteach**... not to be confused with **Samhain** (November). Speaking of which, the Irish for trick or treat is **bob nó bia**.

The Irish for costume or fancy dress is **feisteas** or **culaith**.

I don't want to spoil the fun of anybody who just wants to read adventure stories about druids casting spells and Celtic warriors lobbing each other's heads off. I do want to draw a line between that and the points of Irish history that might be clouded over by it so that everyone can get what they want and we can all get on famously. While I cannot wait to tell my daughter stories of the fierce and fabulous women of Irish mythology and history for her to look up to, I also want to be able to tell her about the work of centuries that it took to get to the certainties we all accept today. In particular, I want to tell her about the hard-won laws and rights she now has.

BREHON LAW,
BUNREACHT LAW

～⌒

The legal system of pre-Strongbow Ireland is fascinating in its sophistication and intricacy, especially
given that court cases in parts of continental Europe were
putting animals on trial for crimes at the time.* However,
some of the fascination with Brehon Law
hinges on an overly forgiving belief that it
was very progressive in regard to women's
rights; this is frankly more of a reflection on
twentieth-century Ireland.

* For more on
this fascinating
area, check out
*The Criminal
Prosecution and
Capital Punishment
of Animals*, E. P.
Evans, 1906.

The Irish Constitution, Bunreacht na Éireann, has been out of fashion with some on
account of a handful of articles which reflect
widespread opinions from the time it was
written, and has been subject to a busy schedule of amendments and attempted amendments in the past quarter
century. At the time of writing, there have been thirty-six
proposed amendments to it; compare this to thirty-three

proposed amendments to the American Constitution, which is 150 years older.

I referred to various matters relating to the Irish Constitution in *Motherfoclóir* and don't intend to repeat myself, beyond reminding readers that it's written in both Irish and English, and where there's a difference the Irish version is favoured. In this chapter, I'd like to look at some of the interesting points of the Irish constitution and consider how they were addressed in Brehon Law.

Has it all been progress? The short answer is yes.

AIRTEAGAL 2

Tá gach duine a shaolaítear in oileán na hÉireann, ar a n-áirítear a oileáin agus a fharraigí, i dteideal, agus tá de cheart oidhreachta aige nó aici, a bheith páirteach i náisiún na hÉireann. Tá an teideal sin freisin ag na daoine go léir atá cáilithe ar shlí eile de réir dlí chun bheith ina saoránaigh d'Éirinn. Ina theannta sin, is mór ag náisiún na hÉireann a choibhneas speisialta le daoine de bhunadh na hÉireann atá ina gcónaí ar an gcoigríoch agus arb ionann féiniúlacht agus oidhreacht chultúir dóibh agus do náisiún na hÉireann.

ARTICLE 2

It is the entitlement and birthright of every person born in the island of Ireland, which includes its islands and seas, to be part of the Irish Nation. That is also the entitlement of all persons otherwise qualified in accordance with law to be citizens of Ireland. Furthermore, the Irish nation cherishes its special affinity with people of Irish ancestry living abroad who share its cultural identity and heritage.

The area of citizenship is one of the most obvious points of progress in Ireland since the Brehon Law age. Rather than having a one-person, one-vote system, Brehon society was divided into ranks, ranging from **rí ruireach** (supreme king) to **mug** (male slave) – and that was just the men. A female slave, a **cumal**, had no rank and her societal value was very much linked to the men she was connected with through parenthood or marriage.

Societal value was expressed through the concept of the honour price, a set value linked to your social rank that was owed to you by someone who wronged you. Cheerfully, there were a number of circumstances where a person's rank could drop but very few where it could rise.

AIRTEAGAL 7

An bhratach trí dhath i uaine, bán, agus flannbhuí, an suaitheantas náisiúnta.

ARTICLE 7

The national flag is the tricolour of green, white and orange.

Flags don't feature much in Brehon Law, but some scholars have suggested that restrictions on particular colours of clothing to certain social ranks would have been in place. This law may have been overstated in primary school stories about Saint Brigid daring to wear more than one colour at a Kildare banquet; it may have been more frowned upon than punished, as the texts very much see misbehaviour in the context of the offended party rather than the offender, and it's unclear who would be injured by seeing a male slave in a fabulous rainbow robe. As for the Irish flag, note the Irish words used for green and orange: **uaine** (true green), rather than **glas** (more appropriate to a vegetable); and **flannbhuí** (**flann** meaning blood-red and **buí** meaning yellow), rather than **oráiste** (more appropriate to a fruit).

AIRTEAGAL 9.1.3

Ní cead náisiúntacht agus saoránacht Éireann a cheilt ar dhuine ar bith toisc gur fireann nó toisc gur baineann an duine sin.

ARTICLE 9.1.3

No person may be excluded from Irish nationality and citizenship by reason of the sex of such person.

This article doesn't come up in conversation very often beyond the fact it has a very, very slight difference between the Irish and English wording – 'by reason of the sex of such person' in English but '*toisc gur fireann nó toisc gur baineann an duine sin*' (on account of the person being male or female) in Irish. Many of you will shrug at the difference, but others might ask if this paragraph could be cited in an attempt to discriminate against gender queer and non-binary people who do not identify as one of the two genders specified.

Such a question raises an important point about the Bunreacht – the entire document is intended to be interpreted as a whole and picking out sub-paragraphs out of context to draw elaborate conclusions just isn't on. In this instance, an attempt to pass a law denying citizenship to non-binary people would flout several other fundamental laws – Article 2, for example. The precedent of the president being referred to as 'he' even though two women have filled that role would also come to bear.

Non-conformity to gender roles doesn't come up much in Brehon Law, which is not to say that it doesn't turn up in literature of the time – most famously the *Táin*, when the Red Branch Knights were 'subject to the pains of women'.

AIRTEAGAL 41.4

Féadfaidh beirt, gan beann ar a ngnéas, conradh pósta a dhéanamh de réir dlí.

ARTICLE 41.4

Marriage may be contracted in accordance with law by two persons without distinction as to their sex.

The Irish word **nead** means nest. It's used figuratively to refer to one's home or marriage in the phrase **do choillis mo nead** (you committed adultery with my wife). **Coillim**, in addition to meaning violate, can also mean castrate.

Article 41.4 is, at the time of writing, the outcome of our most recent constitutional amendment which passed after the 2015 Marriage Referendum.* The key difference between this article and marriage in the Brehon age isn't what you first think – it's actually the number two.

Polygamy was quite widespread in Old Ireland. A man's first or main wife was his **cétmuinter**, and his subsequent wife was his **adaltrach** or **dormun**. Since the removal of civil partnerships, there is only one type of legal 'active'† union in modern Irish law. Brehon distinguishes nine categories of union depending on the relative social status of the partners involved; some of these categories of union are of a casual nature.

---

* The repeal of the 8th Amendment has been voted for but not yet signed at the time of writing.

† In direct contrast to Brehon Law, it is former relationships that are carefully defined in modern Ireland on account of elaborate tax and divorce laws.

AIRTEAGAL 12.10.1

Féadfar an tUachtarán a tháinseamh as ucht mí-iompair a luafar.

ARTICLE 12.10.1

The President may be impeached for stated mis-behaviour.

The Irish for presidential is **uachtaránúil**, not to be confused with **uachtar, arán, úll** which means cream, bread, apple. Despite being considered a ceremonial function compared to the head-of-government job, the role of president is described in far more detail in the constitution than the role of Taoiseach. Much of this is because the job has been designed specifically to make a military coup or dictatorship as hard as possible to occur – understandable in a document written in 1930s Europe.

The constitution doesn't go into depth about what should be considered 'stated misbehaviour', as this detail would be expected to be found in legislation. We do have some details regarding the stated misbehaviours of a king in the Brehon age, though.

Much was expected of kings, as certain breaches of decorum could shatter the illusion of their superiority. This wasn't for their benefit, of course; the king's ability to raise an army and defend his kingdom and subjects hinged on the belief that he was supposed to be their king, a belief that might not be sustained if you had seen him making an eejit of himself recently. No royal credibility meant no military and civil loyalty, which meant no protection from outside threats. Such a failing by a king could be seen as a **d'innchomarta ármuig** – an omen of slaughter.

There were certain things expected of a Brehon king. He had to:

- always travel with a retinue of soldiers;
- not lose in battle;

- not be seen to do any manual labour;

- have no blemishes on his body;*

- not tolerate any satire; and

- obey the laws he set or enforced.

It could be hard to keep up with all these at all times. Fortunately, a legal loophole was available, one replicated by presidents and prime ministers the world over since. A king could appoint one of his underlings to be an **aiteach fortha** (Fergus Kelly translates this as 'substitute churl') who could stand trial on his behalf. This meant justice could be served without compromising the king's royal mystique. Naturally, the **aiteach fortha** would be expected to pay the appropriate fines or receive the appropriate punishment if the king was indeed found guilty.

---

* A wound on the back or the back of the neck was particularly shameful, as it was a mark of cowardly retreat. This was unless the king could prove that the wound was received while heroically charging into enemy troops, taking the risk of a blow from behind.

AIRTEAGAL 29.2

Dearbhaíonn Éire fós gur mian léi go ndéanfaí gach achrann idir náisiúin a réiteach go síochánta le headráin idirnáisiúnta nó le cinneadh breithiúnach.

Ireland affirms its adherence to the principle of the pacific settlement of international disputes by international arbitration or judicial determination.

A **bánchath** is a bloodless battle. The Republic of Ireland is sincerely proud of its tradition of military neutrality and peacekeeping work around the world, which is in contrast to the tradition of military service in Irish communities abroad, especially in the US. Irish vocabulary from the Brehon period suggests that an adherence to the principle of pacific settlement had not yet arrived:

Imghoin can mean slaying, battle or wounding.

Aircet Échta means silver taken as spoils from someone you have slain.

Saithe saighead is an alliterative reference to a shower of arrows.

Lann can mean land, property... or blade. To stain a weapon with blood is **iann a chorcrú** – literally, to purple a blade.

AIRTEAGAL 41.2.1

Go sonrach, admhaíonn an Stát go dtugann an bhean don Stát, trína saol sa teaghlach, cúnamh nach bhféadfaí leas an phobail a ghnóthú dá éagmais. Uime sin, féachfaidh an Stát lena chur in áirithe nach mbeidh ar mháithreacha clainne, de dheasca uireasa, dul le saothar agus faillí a thabhairt dá chionn sin ina ndualgais sa teaghlach.

In particular, the State recognises that by her life within the home, woman gives to the State a support without which the common good cannot be achieved. The State shall, therefore, endeavour to ensure that mothers shall not be obliged by economic necessity to engage in labour to the neglect of their duties in the home.

With its patronizing tone and sexist implications, this is one of the more controversial parts of the Bunreacht; and yet it has been cited in defence of progressive measures like maternity leave without overriding the other guarantees of equality in the text. The Republic can only change the constitution through a referendum, one in which both sides are entitled to similar access to state broadcasting. This means making small tweaks to the wording is extremely difficult, allowing imperfect subparagraphs to fester.

Home life in the age of Brehon Law was subject to different pressures and priorities but the law was child centred and without a blanket assumption that childcare was a woman's role.

For example, a father was solely responsible for the upkeep of a child conceived by wrongdoing. This could include the disapproval of the mother's family, the seduction of another man's wife and much worse. Fathers were also legally obliged to step up if the child's mother was unwell, an outcast or (you guessed it) a satirist. However, given that male satirists were also deemed unsuitable

child-carers, it's unclear who minded the kid when both
parents were that way inclined.

In a way it is fitting that we should wind down here,
noting how the well-being of the child is the centre of a
happy society and reflecting on the role of fathers in this
process. It is fitting that we consider the long journey from
words for blood on a sword up to the modern era of words
for baby monitors and soothers, with a living, changing
language linking the two.

I'm old enough to have friends and colleagues who are
roughly as close in age to Lasairíona as they are to me. It's
strange to think that a lot of the politics and art we found
edgy and progressive in the nineties is considered offen-
sively conservative now. It's disconcerting to think of the
social niceties that have been rendered obsolete and the
new ones that have formed without any central authority
deciding what they should be.

And it's fascinating to see what's happening with language – the changes in slang, in considerate vocabulary,
the way technology changes us and the way it finds a way
of staying the same.

CONCLUSION

Stepping on Lego

~~❧~~

Before I became a father, I imagined that changing nappies and doing night feeds would be massively unpleasant inconveniences, but they really weren't. Those quiet moments at four in the morning listening to her guzzling her little bottle were some of the most peaceful of my whole life. As I rocked from side to side with her in my arms I thought about the lovely, recherché term **réim-chion**, meaning the sway of love. It was no inconvenience at all.

Then one day, quite unplanned and completely against the run of play, I stood on a small plastic toy, not unlike a brick of Lego, with my bare foot. I screamed and swore and screamed some more at the unfairness, the pain, the surprise, the pent-up rage – it all got out. After my wife checked to see if I had been murdered and found out that I had not, she shook a disappointed head and I had a revelation about pain and damage.

Pain isn't damage. Paper cuts hurt as badly as they do

because they don't cut you deep enough for your body to release calming endorphins, so they hurt more than some wounds that damage your body more. Damage isn't pain. You can wreak all kinds of destruction upon yourself without even feeling discomfort – at least not in the moment itself.

Standing on Lego is the distillation of so much of the early years of parenthood – you run around from one chore to the next in your bare feet and get stopped in your tracks by a bullet of pure pain right through your foot. You are reminded that your personal space is her playground now, and she has decorated it with unhatched capsules of pure agony. You seethe in rage at the careless brat who left her toy lying there, but then you remember that the day will come, sooner than you know, that there will be no toys around at all. Your foot still works, and for a few days you tiptoe around a bit more carefully. You have survived to tell the tale. You miss her though she's still here. Pain enters quickly and leaves slowly.

The real inconvenience, where the damage seems to happen, is all in the comparing game. That starts with the crèche drop-offs and pick-ups when you notice that a little girl the same age as yours has passed a milestone already. Then another kid does it, and then another. You have no idea what normal is and what to expect from your own child. You can't help but compare.

You manage to secure an evening to grab a pint or two, and you meet another dad. He asks how your kid is doing; you're polite. He tells you about special savings accounts and additional speech and language services, and you feel massively inadequate. He tells you about the car seat he's just bought and how it's the only one you can trust to not explode. He mentions a training course for parents. It's on mid-week so you won't be able to attend, but that seems to be no problem for him. The comparing game has a senior round too.

You bump into neighbours, former colleagues, people who don't know yet, and they make an off-hand comment about how she'll definitely be going to the Gaelscoil. You remember the night before she was born and the night itself. You feel some of the pain that couldn't fit in your heart that night.

You take her to the hospital for a check-up, never entirely sure if this time is the time you've always been dreading. You get in the lift and someone asks you to hold the door. Another parent comes in with a far, far sicker child and you feel like a monster for worrying as much as you do. You take no pleasure in the comparing game from the other side. You don't want to be grateful that you're not them.

You go online and you scroll absent-mindedly, wondering what everyone is angry about today. Then she grabs the phone off you with her little hands, switching deftly between apps, a person who has never known a world without these devices.

I think about how when my father was a little boy, there were old people in his town who had been alive during the Famine. Their hands had touched his hands. His hands had held mine. Now I hold hers. The old Irish word **béoaigidir** means to make alive or bring back to life. Standing on Lego has hurt me but it has not stopped me. And no childhood is complete without some Lego – building, destroying and rebuilding with only the rules you set yourself.

The only way to beat the comparing game is to stand back – way back – and look at how far you've come and who's joined you along the way.

Nothing compares to that.